Helmut Eller

The Four Temperaments

Helmut Eller

The Four Temperaments

Suggestions for Teachers

Waldorf Publications

Printed with support from the Waldorf Curriculum Fund

Published by
Waldorf Publications at the
Research Institute for Waldorf Education
351 Fairview Avenue, Unit 625
Hudson, NY 12534

ISBN #978-1-943582-18-1
© 2018 Waldorf Publications

Title: *The Four Temperaments: Suggestions for Teachers*
Author: Helmut Eller
Translator: Cynthia Eller
Copy editor: Melissa Merkling
Layout: Ann Erwin
Photographs: Charlotte Fischer
with permission from Verlag Freies Geistesleben

Contents

Preface

A decade after the publication of Peter Lipps' comprehensive study, *The Temperaments and Education: A Portrayal for Lessons at the Waldorf School*,[1] it may seem a bit risky for the publisher to present a book on the same topic. But the central role in Waldorf education played by the question of the temperaments and of teaching according to the temperaments justifies the publisher's courage. This is particularly the case since, in his decades-long profession as class teacher at a Hamburg Waldorf School, author Helmut Eller has been able to amass extensive experience in dealing with diverse aspects of the temperaments in his encounters with children and adults.

He has continued to deepen his study as lecturer at the University of Hamburg, as an instructor in Waldorf teacher trainings and in countless lectures and courses in Germany and abroad. His lively descriptions will inspire teachers' imaginations to take wing while preparing their lessons. His descriptions can also encourage any adult entrusted with the task of teaching to venture forth on the path to self-education into his or her own spiritual province colored by the temperaments.

This last aspect is especially significant for the educator: Education is first and foremost *relationship*, and the question of whether one understands a child the way he is can be answered only if one understands oneself. For what really is effective in a teaching relationship is not what one *knows*, intends or wants to do, but what one *is*, and with what expectations one encounters the children. In connection with their studies of children's temperaments, North American researchers such as Alexander

Thomas, Stella Chess and others have determined how teachers' attitudes are influenced when they feel that temperaments play an important role in assessing children: There were quantifiable retroactive effects on children's achievements. Swiss psychologist Marcel R. Zentner considers it important "that teachers thus learn to recognize temperament differences in their students so they can appropriately develop differentiated forms of teaching and of dealing with students and avoid incorrect judgments that result when the temperament is not taken into consideration." (*The Rediscovery of the Temperaments. An Introduction to Research into Children's Temperaments*, Frankfurt, 1998, p. 124f).

This is exactly the path chosen by the founder of Waldorf education, Rudolf Steiner. On the first day of the preparatory course for the teachers of the first Waldorf school on August 21, 1919, he spoke about a way that a useful relationship can be built up with the children; he called it "the most important task of the educator and teacher" to really know the four temperaments. (Later he went on to develop further viewpoints concerning a dynamic, individualizing knowledge of man.) In a wide range of observations he called attention to the temperaments from the anthroposophical point of view as opposed to the classical theory of the temperaments. And from these viewpoints he developed methods and directions for effectively and beneficially dealing with the individual child while teaching a large class by employing a variety of methods. In other words, he presented ways of individualizing while teaching, by taking the child's temperament into consideration. This is an extremely important viewpoint and—despite critical voices that surface periodically decrying the dangers of stereotyping as a result of temperament education—it indeed justifies the fact that paying attention to the temperaments, right down to the seating order in a class, still plays an important role in the Waldorf school day! It is the individualized view that makes all the difference: A pedagogy like Waldorf education can foster development only if the relationship between child and educator is constantly examined, clarified and created anew: in short, only if it is alive.

In times like ours, in which centralized educational standards, high-stakes testing and the like are favored over any individual learning process, it is especially important to call attention again and again to this fundamental tenet of Waldorf education. For that reason we hope that this book by Helmut Eller will open eyes in this regard and also arouse the desire to deal always with the individual characteristics of all children, including the teaching methods that best suit their needs.

– Walter Riethmüller
Stuttgart, August 2007

1. Introduction

It is not uncommon to hear someone described as "temperamental." In German one would say *temperamentvoll*: lively, vivacious, "full of temperament." And we all feel we know what is meant by this. When we want to express the opposite, we might say, "She is sooo phlegmatic!" The first description expresses simultaneous amazement, recognition and admiration, while the second invokes one of the four classical temperaments, with somewhat derogatory overtones—mistaken ones, as we shall discover. So we see here only a polarity: Either someone has temperament or s/he has none.

The classical four temperaments—sanguine, phlegmatic, choleric and melancholic—were first recognized by the Greek physician Hippocrates (460–377 BC), who treated them on the basis of his humoral pathology (*humores* = elemental fluids of the body). He also made medical connections to the four elements of Empedocles (490–430 BC): fire, air, water, earth. Finally, it was Aristotle who expanded this topic to include the four qualities: warm, cold, dry, damp. In ancient times, these connections had significance primarily in the realm of medicine.

In the late Middle Ages it was Dante's teacher Brunetto Latini, among others, and in the 18th/19th centuries, Immanuel Kant and the poet Novalis who again dealt with this topic and considered it deeply significant. But it was not until the winter of 1798/99 that the German writers Goethe and Schiller succeeded in discovering the first really practical approach and recorded it in the form of the colorful "temperament rose," which is still a great help when it comes to practicing self-education and understanding other people.

In 1919 with the founding of the Waldorf School, Rudolf Steiner took things one step further, using the theory of the temperaments for the benefit of education. In so doing, he applied the familiar terminology of Hippocrates, but not his theory of the four humors. Rather, he created a completely new, much more extensive basis of knowledge through his research and conclusions in the realm of spiritual science, resulting in a wealth of possibilities for applying the temperament theory in practical daily life, as well as in recognizing and understanding our fellow human beings and the world. To illustrate this is one of my aims in this book.

For almost a hundred years, Rudolf Steiner's indications have been taken up and tested in Waldorf schools around the world. Now, after numerous colleagues have published their experiences (notably Peter Lipps in his extensive work *Temperaments and Education*[1]), it is my objective—by means of fourfold descriptions "colored by the temperaments"—to stimulate the reader to inwardly slip into each temperament so as to understand it actively, and then learn to interact with it. To help the reader experience various text passages in the style typical of each temperament, I have employed four different kinds of punctuation.

The fact that in every person all four temperaments are present calls upon us to actually look for and discover all four. It will become obvious that one or two, sometimes even three, may appear more strongly; that they blend together; that they represent deep-seated habits; that they are a part of our nature, but colored by our own individuality so as to distinguish ourselves from every other person. And since two people can never be exactly alike, I hope my explanations will help dispel and put to rest all clichés and stereotypes.

Right from the outset we should comment on the expressions "the choleric," "the phlegmatic," and so forth. It has become common, when talking about the temperaments to characterize people in this way, although we all possess all four tendencies. So it would be more accurate to say: "The child or person whose choleric (or phlegmatic, etc.) characteristics particularly stand out, attract attention or predominate..." But how unwieldy for both author and reader. Therefore I hope my readers will understand that, to simplify matters and for the sake of the narrative flow, I will speak of "the choleric," "the sanguine," etc., but that, I will always mean the *person* in which a particular temperament appears more strongly than the other three.

The works of Rudolf Steiner are the basis for all concepts dealing with the study of the human being in understanding the significance of the temperaments and dealing with them in daily life. After an initial observation of certain phenomena, I will therefore explain several basic concepts of his view of the human being. To the reader who is able to relate to this manner of viewing a person, unexpected possibilities will present themselves for seeing ourselves, our students and each other—and above all our temperaments—in a new light and to understand them more deeply.

I hope that, as we progress on our common path, it will become obvious that what matters in order to slip from one temperament into another is inner mobility and flexibility. May we succeed in achieving a new understanding and ultimately in even being able to love them all! Through observing the temperaments we encounter only a portion of a person, but a very important one.

At this point I would like to heartily thank a number of people without whose help this book would not have materialized. My friend, Rolf Speckner, was the first to look at all my texts and work through them critically, making note of things that needed changing. Mrs. Masayo Toriyama, whose task it was to revise and translate my texts into her mother tongue for the original Japanese publication, frequently posed further stimulating questions that were then also significant for the subsequent German version. I am very grateful to Stefan Leber for reading my manuscript and recommending publication to the Verlag Freies Geistesleben. It was at his suggestion that Walter Riethmüller of the Freie Hochschule for Waldorf Education in Stuttgart checked through the texts and made suggestions for which I am very grateful. He and also Martin Lintz of Verlag Freies Geistesleben, who edited my first book (*The Class Teacher at the Waldorf School*), thankfully saw to it that everything ultimately became ready for publication.

In particular I would now like to thank the American publisher, the Research Institute for Waldorf Education, for its willingness to publish this book, and even greater thanks go to my dear American wife, Cynthia, who so often listened to my lectures on the temperaments and was therefore capable like no other of translating all the details so accurately into her mother tongue.

– Helmut Eller
Hamburg, Fall 2016

2. A First Encounter with the Temperaments

How Children Enter the Classroom

Let's begin by imagining a number of situations in which we observe four different children reacting according to their predominating temperaments. In a later chapter we'll make a similar attempt to learn to recognize the temperaments in adults.

To gain an initial understanding and familiarize ourselves with the temperaments, we'll pick a situation that might occur in the morning before class begins. The reader should try to imagine in as lively a way as possible how a class teacher in one of the lower grades welcomes his students at the classroom door. While reading the four descriptions, try to vividly picture how the four children approach the teacher, shake his hand, look at him, greet him, go to their desks, put down their satchels, take their seats and wait for class to begin.

At my lectures and seminars I try to act out characteristic situations for my listeners to help them envisage different aspects of behavior. Since I can't do that in a book, I've used different kinds of punctuation to try to reflect this: Commas, question marks, dashes or exclamation points should help you actively slip into the children's reactions and experience what is described— though you may have to make a few attempts to get satisfactory results.

Here comes *the first child*! Moves fast down the corridor! Takes brisk, energetic steps! You can hear her coming! Walks straight up to the teacher! Now they meet! Looks her teacher in the eye! Straightforward, effective, intense! Quickly sticks out her hand! A rapid, firm squeeze! Energetic! Straight posture! Says, "Good morning, Mr. Eller!" – succinct, clear, expressive! Then she's off! Heads for new destinations! Marches with resolute steps into the classroom! Okay, now to my seat! Here at last! Down with the satchel! Oh no! That was too fast! Now the strap ripped off again! "Mom's had to sew that on a bunch of times! But she didn't do a good enough job – it's her fault!" Shove the satchel under my desk! "Oh, now I've got to wait! Still have to wait! He still hasn't started teaching! Waiting is all I do! And I don't like to wait! I'm coming later tomorrow!" This might be a child with a lot of choleric characteristics!

A second child approaches: Calmly … at a leisurely pace … swaying a bit from left to right … not at all in a hurry … daydreaming a bit and with a friendly expression … might not even have noticed the teacher standing at the door … turns to him now. Thank goodness he stretches out his hand in time to take mine … The small hand is trustingly placed in the teacher's hand … no noticeable squeeze … without exerting himself, very relaxed … he lifts his head – very calmly … his eyes brighten momentarily – look into those of his teacher … and come to rest there for a moment. A pleasant smile appears on his little face … stays there a while … his greeting is friendly, peaceful … with a gentle look … completely without haste … enjoying this moment, too … his gaze wanders on … his smile fades a bit. Now he heads for his seat … still smiling … he lets his satchel glide down off his shoulders … it lands on the ground … "It's too bad that I couldn't catch it fast enough … sometimes I'm faster … then I can catch it." … So, now it's time to sit down … he hangs his satchel on the side of his desk … "That's easier than having to shove it under my desk." …He then waits patiently until class begins … Ah, here comes his class teacher … who asks him, "And how are you today?"–"Fine." – "Do you like coming to school?"–"Oh, yes." – "Do you like it here?"–"Yes, it's so comfy and cozy here." This child's behavior reveals a lot of the typical characteristics of the phlegmatic.

Wow, here comes *the next one*: Bouncing lightly as she steps, with one of her classmates at her side (now her "best friend" because she's "so nice"), telling her all about her latest experiences (she's experienced so many interesting things since yesterday!). Oho, there's the teacher! Moving nimbly toward him, momentarily interrupting her busy conversation and quickly adding, "You're my new best friend!" – then quickly focusing on the greeting – that's always easy for her. Happily grasping her teacher's hand (touching it fleetingly would be more accurate), beaming and with a short, bright glance into the teacher's eyes, she deftly and cheerfully calls out her greeting! But she's already looking elsewhere, checking out the teacher, seeking and finding: "Oh, did you get a haircut?" "Are those new shoes?" Following a short pause (she was done shaking hands before she started) she suddenly remembers something she needs to report: "I'm supposed to say hi from mommy – and – my dad is feeling better now, he was sooooo sick – and – my hamster nearly died but we nursed him back to health fast!" Now she's quickly off to her seat, but doesn't sit down. She opens her satchel, takes out the invitations to her birthday party and quickly distributes them. (Saying to herself:) "Thank goodness the teacher hasn't started class yet! In 3 weeks it's my birthday – I can hardly wait! I wanted to invite all the kids in the class – I really like them all – but mommy said I could only invite half of them – that would be enough. It was really hard to decide who to invite!" Then quickly back to her seat – the teacher wants to begin class! This is how a child with a primarily sanguine temperament might behave one morning. The next day, though, she will definitely have lots more to talk about.

Taking deliberate, measured steps and consciously observing the situation taking place right now at the classroom door, *another child* approaches whose delicate, sensitive, inquisitive manner is hopefully not being noticed by anyone else. He stops at some distance from the teacher, for he's noticed that his teacher is very preoccupied with (the sanguine) Hannah, and he begins to brood semi-consciously over what he hears: "What is Hannah talking about? Does our teacher like to listen to that? I'm not going over there yet – I don't want to bother him. Hannah is never going to finish. No – I'd rather not say hello to him from *my* mother. Her father was sick? Oh, how terrible. If my father got sick ... he couldn't go to work. Her hamster almost died? If my guinea pig was that sick, I would definitely stay home. No, I couldn't go to school. I really feel sorry for poor Hannah. Okay – now the teacher's finished with her." With alert senses and a willing attitude, he steps toward the teacher. He stretches out his hand carefully, trustingly, grasping cautiously. His serious and questioning gaze meets that of his teacher as he tries to conceal his own inner mood entirely. His voice is a bit muted but very respectful as he greets him, then cautiously withdraws his hand. Turning away, he can be very preoccupied with this encounter: "He gave me such a friendly look again. That makes me feel good. I wonder if he feels sorry for the hamster, and for Hannah? Later on, I'll go over and talk to her. Gee, if my guinea pig got that sick..." He heads for his seat as directly as possible. "I sure hope nobody bumps into me – like what happened last week." He carefully places his satchel underneath his desk so it won't get scratched. "I wonder what Hannah is doing over there? She's still running around the classroom. I certainly wouldn't do that. Oh, she's handing out birthday invitations. So many of the kids are getting one! Why is she inviting Moritz? Yes, Cornelia over there I would invite, too. Did she think of me? If not, I'm never inviting her to my parties again. Oh, Hannah, you did invite me! Thank you so much for letting me come! Oh, class is about to begin. I hope Hannah gets back to her seat in time!" This child is a good example of someone with a lot of melancholic characteristics.

For the sake of emphasis, these situations have naturally been somewhat dramatized at times, and represent only some of the countless possible reactions. But they should provide us with an important first impression and a basis for discovering the distinguishing features, the basic phenomena, of the temperaments, which can in turn serve as the key to all further observations. I have intentionally avoided examples of behavioral extremes, such as the anger of a very choleric person or the indifference of an overly phlegmatic one.

Already at this point it should be stressed again that everyone possesses all four temperaments, but that one temperament, usually two—and sometimes even three—predominate. In addition, different temperaments may mix, and each of us contributes his or her personal shade or hue, which is why no two people can be the same. These topics will be addressed in greater depth later on.

What Their Behaviors Reveal

Now let's try to discover the fundamentals in the above situations. In the first description the short, choppy sentences and exclamation points give you the feeling of how a *choleric* child leads the way, constantly strives forward and energetically pursues her goal! Once it is achieved, she immediately seeks a new one! Determination and drive go hand in hand! We can sense something forceful, energetic, quick-witted, vigorous and decisive! Sheer willpower! Firm *goals* are set and *forcefully* pursued! You get the impression whatever she plans will be carried out tenaciously and thoroughly! These are the splendid characteristics of the choleric temperament. And since each of us has some of this temperament, you could say that it constitutes our active side—while in a choleric, it is strongly pronounced and dominant.

Let's slip inside our choleric. She's reached her goal and must now sit there quietly waiting for class to begin: not exactly easy for her! It's no wonder she gets impatient and reacts by saying, "Tomorrow I'm going to come later!"

The second—*phlegmatic*—child does exactly the opposite. The way he walks, the way he shakes hands, the way he looks at the teacher and his surroundings all reveal the great *composure and calmness* with which he reacts to everything going on around him. He enters the classroom dreamily, with a contented smile, and stays like that while greeting his teacher—and all the way to his seat. He experiences things sentimentally and, whenever possible, comfortably and cozily as well, because he encounters the world around him with a feeling of well-being at his own leisurely, unhurried pace. Nothing can get him worked up. He particularly relishes everything that has to do with regularity and rhythm, which is why he can spend a lot of time doing things he enjoys. His great assets are patience, endurance, calmness and peacefulness. He would never insult anyone. He enjoys situations that make him feel good and has no desire to change them. In all these situations it's easy to see the strong contrasts with the choleric child.

As adults we will be able to discover this temperament in ourselves when we settle down in a cozy corner and make ourselves comfortable, when we relax, get tired, react passively— or get ready for bed.

How different the *sanguine* child is! Light and cheerful, spontaneous and confident, she openly approaches new situations. She channels her attention in a flash toward *new impressions*; she sees and hears everything; her *senses* are wide open and she quickly teams up and allies herself with things and causes she encounters. She makes new friends easily. She is quick to discover something new about her teacher, suddenly remembers all the things she wanted to tell him, bubbles over with the news—then runs away and hands out her birthday invitations. The sanguine child loves the world and other people and would like to embrace everyone. She doesn't want to miss a thing and regrets that she doesn't have eyes in the back of her head. Her diverse interests are stimulating for her, the community and society, which she takes great pleasure in shaping and helping to organize. Her face is an open book that reveals her emotions and inner experiences. She also has her share of troubles and worries, but they only weigh on her for a short time. How she loves everything that's beautiful! Loving and complete devotion in her social life as well as agility of mind and body are her great assets. We can all discover the signs of this temperament in us, for example when marveling at the wonders of nature on a walk, when enjoying the passing scenery from a train window, when shopping or just window-shopping.

The fourth child, with the *melancholic* temperament, behaves the opposite way. He faces the world with caution, inner seriousness and extreme awareness. He has the ability to wait, observe and be seriously concerned about everything, and he approaches other people and the world around him cautiously— just as his meeting with his teacher shows. He showed great compassion when Hannah, the student before him, described the suffering her pet went through. He feels much more at home in his inner world—in his thoughts, emotions and even dreams. He loves inner and outer *peace and quiet* and behaves sensitively and tactfully. He doesn't like bothering other people, which is why he usually keeps to himself. He is a master of self-control and self-criticism. He therefore observes others closely and is capable of suffering deeply with them. His great assets are his ability to think things through seriously and to sympathize and empathize with

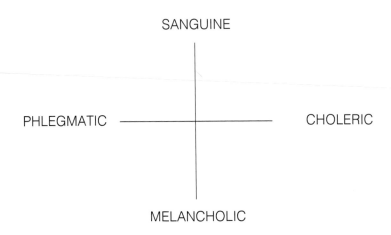

SANGUINE

PHLEGMATIC ———————————— CHOLERIC

MELANCHOLIC

others. He chooses what he observes, pays thorough attention to his impressions and asks himself many questions—from very simple to most profound.

This temperament color is familiar to all of us, as well. Who has never felt melancholy after experiencing troubles or sadness? Even the most sanguine people experience this mood when they lose someone dear to them or when a close friendship ends.

You may have noticed that there are always two temperaments that stand in exact opposition to each other: *choleric* opposite *phlegmatic* and *sanguine* opposite *melancholic*. In the study of the temperaments it's common to represent this foursome in the shape of a cross. My diagram differs from the usual version because I place the sanguine temperament above and the melancholic below. The following study will show how meaningful this arrangement is.

How to Develop an Eye for the Temperaments

Our summary of the basic phenomena, which primarily reflected the temperaments' positive aspects, is by no means complete. Other authors have drawn up lists of further phenomena for each of the temperaments.[2] But this could lead to thinking in stereotypes and using mental checklists to categorize someone whose temperament you want to determine—which a computer could actually do much faster and more efficiently. But this will not lead to a genuine understanding of people! In contrast, I'd like to suggest a method that can lead to a creative and lively way of recognizing and viewing the temperaments, and that goes far beyond using memorized or predetermined checklists.

With the help of the preceding observations, we have discovered two to three basic characteristics for each of the temperaments. These are their particular qualities, revealing something about their essences. It's these we will now take a closer look at—by choosing typical situations in which the four temperaments behave in characteristic ways. In the next chapter we will try to vividly picture and recreate such situations in our minds by more or less slipping into four different children and becoming choleric, phlegmatic, sanguine and melancholic.

This sort of activity can stimulate our creativity and imagination, which is of vital significance for the teacher and therefore extremely important! If you learn to picture and imagine such situations vividly through constant practice, you can learn to "see" the temperaments, and the next morning at the classroom door or in other situations you'll experience exactly what you inwardly prepared yourself to look for. Something of the children's temperaments will reveal itself to you because, through this active, creative practice, you have developed new perceptive abilities. You will see before you what you've learned to "perceive" through your own practice.

A simple example will illustrate how this works: You are waiting for a particular red car on a very busy street. You have an exact inner impression of the make, shape and color, and you continue to wait. You gladly spot a number of cars that look right, but in vain. Finally the right one comes! You get in, sit next to the driver and start a conversation, suddenly noticing that your eye is still busy searching out red cars... but thank goodness, only for a little while.

To develop a good eye for the different temperaments, it's necessary—as with most other things—to practice over and over. Most important of all, our observations should always be carried out in a loving way, never judgmentally. There's also an important difference from the example of the red car: When we encounter people we will always discover something new; we'll learn that each individual displays the basic phenomena summarized above—but that they mix and blend in very individual, never stereotypical nuances. Observing others is therefore always a very rewarding experience, and one can never cease to wonder at the endless variety of ways that the basic characteristics of the four temperaments can be modified.

When we picture the abovementioned life situations, we need a certain amount of fantasy and imagination. If we picture a certain child we think we know well and consider quite choleric, we'll notice that he by no means displays typically choleric behavior in everything he does and on all occasions. Every person contains all four temperaments. So we shouldn't be surprised when a child behaves completely unusually in certain situations and activities—in other words, when he acts out of a different temperament and reacts unexpectedly calmly and phlegmatically.

That's why it's always better to slip into the following descriptions without immediately imagining a specific person.

If you allow yourself to learn and be enriched by exact observation, there's also no danger of sliding into the realm of fantasy. Rather, you gradually begin to develop the capacity for "exact fantasy," as Goethe termed it. I hope the following examples can serve to stimulate the process of practicing this skill.

How Children Act in a Classroom Situation

Let us now observe the behavior of four different children in a classroom situation and then how they come home from school, acting characteristically for each of the temperaments.

Parents and teachers tend to be glad when children raise their hands often to participate actively in class. Is it legitimate to expect this activity in the same way from all children?

Let's imagine the following situation: In geography class the previous day, the teacher vividly described how people live on the Halligs, ten small flat islands without protective dikes off the coast of Schleswig-Holstein in Germany, and how dramatic things can get in a storm tide. Now, the following day, the teacher asks the class: "Who can tell us something about the farmers on the Hallig islands?" Here are the reactions:

Raise my hand fast! Reach my hand way up! Wiggle my index finger! Right in front of the teacher's face is best, so he sees me! Wave my arm back and forth (while repeating to myself): "I want to answer this one!" – He has to pick *me* this time! – But he doesn't! – He doesn't even see me! I know he doesn't! – He always makes me wait to answer! – And now there are so many others raising their hands! What a shame! – No – now he's going to pick me! –

Finally! – Now I can give the answer!—the enthusiastic *choleric* child!

Get a spontaneous idea; just say something – anything; quickly raise my hand; if necessary, wave my arm wildly back and forth; signal the teacher to look at me and smile at him; show him that I've got something interesting to say; shout a short little answer to him in case he looks in a different direction; I'm sure he's always pleased to hear my answers; give a cheerful excuse when he keeps asking us not to shout out answers; if he doesn't pick me, quickly tell my neighbor the answer. If I am picked, bubble over with answers—the multifaceted *sanguine* child.

Feeling good … daydreaming a little … calmly listening to the question … but feeling no urge to answer it … enjoying hearing how well other kids can answer the question … gladly avoiding having to strenuously raise my hand … feeling no need to reveal my abilities … preferring peace and quiet: the *phlegmatic* child. As a teacher one must make a concerted effort to remain conscious of these children during class, waking and stimulating them once in a while to ask a direct question. You'll be surprised at the good answers you'll get! Even if they're daydreaming, such children emotionally grasp and take in the content of lessons that are taught actively and artistically.

Not wanting to answer right away, instead saying to himself, "First I'll let the others answer – I don't even like thinking about that terrible storm tide the teacher described – the poor islanders: They almost lost their lives! – What could I say? – It would have to be something serious and important (I love difficult questions) – oh yes, that's it: They were all rescued by a lucky stroke of fate – even the animals – but how should I express that? – I'll raise my hand – but cautiously: Now I'm raising my hand, preferably only halfway – I'm not really sure my answer's correct – it would actually be best if the teacher didn't pick me to answer." "Oh – he did notice me after all – now I've got to go through with it."—the *melancholic* child.

Coming Home from School

How differently these children come home from school! Let's take a look at how they approach the door, ring the doorbell and then have to wait a minute because their mother is on the phone and can't come right away.

The *choleric* child marches briskly toward the door! – forcefully rings the doorbell! – with his thumb, of course! – and once again! "Where is she? She's not answering!" – Leans on the doorbell! Again! – "Oh, she's on the phone! Why does she have to use the phone so much? Doesn't she have anything else to do? – Well, finally!"

Stepping merrily, hopping cheerfully—perhaps whistling or singing—the *sanguine* child approaches the door; rings the bell with his pointer finger, pressing it in short, rhythmic beats: Then his mother will know and be happy that's it's him at the door. "She's not coming – well, it doesn't matter. Ah, I can hear her on the phone. I guess I'll take a look at our flower beds while I'm waiting. Oh, there's a butterfly, and over there's a little bee!" His mother appears at the door: "Mommy, come over here – look what I've found!"

Not at all in a hurry, a bit late, strolling along leisurely, stopping to rest once in a while – the *phlegmatic* child comes home and positions herself in front of the door – and rings the bell – once is enough. "Mom's probably on the phone ... no problem ... she'll let me in as soon as she can ... whenever she's done ... sometimes that takes a while … but that's okay … I'll just sit down here on the stoop for a while … and wait … and make myself comfortable … till she comes."

With measured steps, a bit lost in thought and recalling how a boy beat up another boy at school earlier – which she'll definitely have to tell her mom about – the *melancholic* child approaches the door. "I wonder if Mommy's home?" – now ringing the bell gently so she doesn't shock her – "What's wrong? – Why doesn't she answer? Is she sick? – Has something happened to her? That would be awful! I heard about a kid who went to visit his grandma and rang the doorbell until the neighbor lady came and told him that his grandma'd been taken to the hospital! If something like that happened to Mommy … wait – isn't that her voice? … Ah, so she's on the phone … thank goodness … then I won't bother her … just yesterday she told me that I'm always so sensitive … that's how I always want to be."

Drawing an Island Scene

Children's temperaments are also reflected in the way they draw. This can be seen in the four crayon drawings reproduced on pages 32–33, which were done during a fifth-grade geography block to illustrate the discussion of "a storm tide on the Halligs," the coastal islands. The children were told how the little flat islands with their raised earth mounds are flooded during storm tides, and how the waves break against the doors of the houses. The islanders and their animals are thus in great danger and might even have to try to save themselves by climbing to the top floor, if the breakers are threatening to crash through the walls below them. The top floors are safer because the houses' thick vertical posts are firmly anchored deep in the earth so they can withstand the force of the sea.

Now let's take a look at the pictures the children drew. After a first look that might make us chuckle here and there, we'll attempt to recreate the drawing process the children went through.

The first picture was drawn by a girl. Let's try to imagine how she drew it. She began on the reverse side of the paper by drawing the big man-made earth mound. Too big, much too big! Turn the paper over! Draw the mound again – press down hard on the crayons! Okay, now it's nice and green! Now a big sturdy house on top! Stone walls and big wooden beams! Oh, I forgot the windows! I'll draw them right in the stone walls! Ooops! I forgot the house door! Well, that's okay, the door is at the back of the house! A sturdy thatched roof! Now the waves – coming from all different directions – one reaches the house! Now the dark blue sky! Whoops – the clouds are missing! Black over the blue! Can't forget the lightning bolts: I'll use yellow to draw a thick zigzag line through the blue! Oh, yellow and blue make green! What? Green lightning bolts? Impossible! I'll cover them over with red! So – now all that's missing is my name on the back – I'll write it real big right across the first mound I drew! Unmistakable: a *choleric* young lady!

Now let's attempt to see things from the *sanguine* child's viewpoint and experience the way he draws. What is going through his head? "In the foreground you've got to see water (after all, it is an island!) … the people living there need water, too … they collect the rainwater (the ocean is salty) … so they need a well (he forgot that it's really a collecting pool)… so they also need a device to pull up the water … behind that, the earth mound in various shades of green … now the house … a lot of thin beams and small bricks; blue, red, purple windows (they want to be able to see what's going out outside!); a yellow door ... then the roof (so thin and jutting out so far that the next storm will rip it right off) ... now a big sturdy chimney (air is his element) ... and in front of the house a slender stoop, a delicate bench ... now on the left a koog (a fenced-in piece of land that's been reclaimed from the sea) ... (he notices that this looks funny): I'm going to label it "Koog" so people can tell what it is ... now a tiny little red house ... (The paper had slipped out of position while he was drawing it; when he straightened out the page:) "Oops, that house is tipped over ... oh, well, it doesn't matter ... but how lonely to live all alone on a Hallig! No, I'll add another little island over here on the right ... It's within waving distance for me ... and if somebody wants to come over from there and visit, he can moor his boat on this mooring post (in the right foreground) ... So now here comes the water ... a lot of waves, all different kinds ... one crashes up onto the island (like a delicate curl) ... ships in the background ... a sailboat, fully rigged (in the middle of a storm!) ... down below are the portholes (so he can look out when he's below deck) ... lightning bolts strike another ship ... gee, this is fun! ... there's still room up at the top of the page ... a good spot for more lightning bolts ... I'll add a few there."

The next picture can show what it's like when a *melancholic* mood prevails. "First I'll use my favorite colors: dark green and dark blue...I'll start at the bottom of the paper – that's probably best...carefully draw the first wave into the corner ... with slanted edges and pointy on top ... so it looks like a triangle ... now the other waves next to it and above it: They should all look pretty much the same ... because of their pointy tops all my waves look like they've been whipped up by the storm." (That they look like mountains, she didn't notice. The close connection between this temperament and the earth element with its crystalline forms is reflected here in an interesting way.) "So, now I'll draw my house, the kind of house I'd like to live in someday ... isolated and alone ... but with my parents and brothers and sisters, of course ... way up high above the raging water ... a big, wide house ... I have to draw the half-timbering and the windows very exactly so the house doesn't topple over in the storm ... I'll put three chimneys on my house so it's warm in every room ... now I can feel really safe and cozy in there. – Oh, but everything in my picture looks so calm ... maybe I'd better draw in one dangerous, pouncing wave ... I'll put it up here on the right (it looks like a big curl) ... not too close to the house, because I don't want anything to happen to it, and besides – there are people and animals inside! ... and now the gray sky, and the sun should shine through a little bit ... even though there's a storm."

Now we'll let the last picture transport us into the peace-loving mood of the *phlegmatic* child. When I met the boy who drew this many years later—we have since developed a very close, warm friendship—I showed him this picture, and he could clearly recall how he went about drawing it: Calmly ... beginning in the middle of the page ... way over on the left ... first a little island ... plain and green ... a red house ... leave openings for the windows ... then they'll look bright ... that's also the easiest way to draw them ... now move on to the right ... the island and house a little bigger ... and the next island ... the island green, the house red ... and the next island ... a whole row of islands ... from small to large ... everything is peaceful, everything is calm ... (what beautiful use of color! The complementary colors red and green!) ... now draw in the ocean below the islands ... a nice round wave ... then another one ... wave after wave ... now the next row: wave ... wave ... row after row ... fill up all the space ... right down to the bottom ... now only the ocean in the background is missing ...

The choleric child experiences the storm-tide as powerful and dynamic.

The sanguine child draws his picture colorfully and with a lot of various details.

The melancholic child's portrayal is well thought through and systematic.

The phlegmatic child draws a peaceful ocean with calm symmetry and regularity.

the setting sun … its reflection in the water … the evening sky … there, that's it … wait – write the title on the back of the page … "What was it again? … oh, right – now I remember…" He writes "Storm tide" and his name.

These drawings reflect in a very typical way much of what this study of the temperaments is trying to sharpen our awareness for. At the same time they can serve as an impetus for teachers to look at their students' drawings in a new light to discover the nuances of their temperaments.

3. The Basics for Understanding the Temperaments

Up to now we've tried to get a feel for each of the four temperaments by imagining certain situations—without being familiar with temperament theory. This is what we will now address. It will gradually lead us to a deeper understanding of the phenomena described so far. First of all, it's important to know how the temperaments mix with each other.

How the Temperaments Mix

From the diagram on page 22 we can see that pairs of temperaments stand in opposition to one another. Since every one of us has something of each temperament, it frequently happens that two or three of them blend together. The diagram with added connecting lines (to the right) can help clarify which ones mix together.

As the curved lines indicate, each temperament can mix with its two neighbors, and the combinations are then referred to as melancholic-choleric, melancholic-phlegmatic, sanguine-choleric, etc. The predominant temperament is mentioned first.

For example, if we have a child with a *sanguine-choleric* combination, we'll recognize on the one hand her nimble agility, cheerfulness and openness to the world around her, and on the other hand the fact that she can display determination and drive as a result of her choleric tendency.

It can also happen that *both* the temperament's neighbors show up, so that, for instance, sanguine characteristics mix with both choleric and phlegmatic traits. In such a child we can observe that a melancholic, serious state of mind with its tendency toward introversion and thoughtful reflection is present least of all.

Now we may ask, is a *sanguine-melancholic* combination possible? And could *choleric* and *phlegmatic* tendencies mix? Yes, both are possible and indeed occur very often in life, although they are such extremely different temperaments!

However, we really shouldn't think of these as "mixtures," because a sanguine-melancholic person cannot simultaneously be cheerful and bubbly with exuberance and love of life while dealing seriously with vital questions and sympathy for a sick neighbor! These temperaments may manifest one after the other

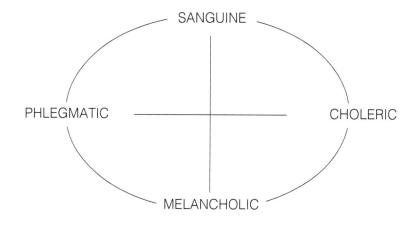

in time: First one is in evidence, then the other. This also holds true for the other opposite temperaments, choleric and phlegmatic.

To give us an even more vivid idea of these combinations, another representation will be explored later (page 51): the "temperament rose" of Goethe and Schiller, which provides each temperament with two more possibilities of mixing with its neighbors, giving rise to a twelve-part rose.

If we succeed in mastering our dominant temperament and all its nuances from the very depths of our personality, our ego, then we can recognize the basic phenomena we have spoken of—colored somewhat differently for each individual. But what happens if we cannot fully master our temperament, or do so only partially, if it more or less slips out of our ego's control—which is something we can imagine happening in many instances?

To better understand this topic, we should first turn our attention to the origins of temperament theory, which date back to the time of the Greeks.

Hippocrates and His Theory

The Greek physician Hippocrates (460–377 BC), for whom the Hippocratic oath is named, was the first to observe the abovementioned phenomena in his patients. On the basis of the extreme forms of the temperaments, described later (page 45), he arrived at the surprising conclusion that they corresponded to four different internal fluid currents (*humors* = fluids), which in turn related to internal organs. He also incorporated into his theory the four elements discovered by Empedocles.

Hippocrates recognized a connection between the choleric temperament and the gallbladder (Greek: *chole* = gall). This seems logical—and here we'll jump ahead to the next chapter—if we consider that an excessively choleric person is prone to anger. In German there's even the saying, "His gallbladder is running over," to describe someone livid with rage. Someone whose face grows visibly pale during an outburst of temper might even take on a light-green hue; this is caused by the gall backing up!

In a melancholic person (*melan* = black), Hippocrates referred to a thickened stream of gall that grows black because of its sluggishness. This, too, is plausible: The melancholic person has a strong inclination to thinking and reflection, and it's more difficult for him to become active and do practical work. If the choleric owes his drive to his gallbladder, it's logical that the melancholic's thickened stream of gall will spoil his pleasure in putting something into practice.

The sanguine temperament (*sanguis* = blood) has an inner connection with our living, flowing blood. Here Hippocrates can only have meant the fresh, oxygenated blood that flows ceaselessly through the aorta into the circulatory system, branches out further and further in the arteries and ultimately reaches the periphery in the system of tiny veins. Here we should imagine a sanguine child, how she shows a keen interest in everything around her, how she wants to go everywhere and loves the world wholeheartedly—an image that speaks for itself.

Hippocrates saw a connection between the phlegmatic temperament and all the fluid processes in the body that are not connected with particular organs. Here we could perhaps cite the glandular system, as well as the lymph and other fluids that constantly flow through the body and serve as the basis of our life processes. The Greek word *phlegma* means "phlegm" or "mucus," which, however, has a somewhat different meaning in our language. We can sense that these watery processes have a connection to the peace-loving phlegmatic person.

In summary, we could say that Hippocrates' way of observing the temperaments focused on four different fluid streams that can be found in all of us. These processes interpenetrate and spread through each other, and—depending on the strength of the individual streams—a certain shade or hue will predominate. They combine with each other, and Hippocrates considered this mixture crucial. We should therefore not really be surprised when we hear that he chose the word *temperament* because it means "mixture." But instead of speaking of "liquids," he used the word *humors*, which means "fluids." So it is entirely legitimate to refer to Hippocrates' "theory of vital fluids."

The Temperaments and the Elements of Empedocles

We have the Greek physician and philosopher Empedocles (490–430 BC) to thank for the theory of the four elements. Over the centuries, noteworthy personalities embraced his insights and expanded upon them, until they were finally pushed into the background by modern science and ultimately became a target of ridicule.

Hippocrates took up the ideas of his older contemporary and at once linked the four elements—fire, air, water and earth—to the four temperaments. Even today this application can contribute to an easier understanding of the temperaments.

When the Greeks spoke of the elements, they meant an invisible entity that stood behind everything visible and could assume the most diverse forms in the world. For example, by the concept "water" they understood anything that is or can be fluid, whether in the ocean, in lakes, rivers, streams, rain or dew. But mercury belonged to this category, too. And these elements had both physical and spiritual qualities.

Instead of beginning this analysis with Hippocrates' list, let's ask ourselves: Which temperament has a special relationship with the element of fire, of warmth? Let's imagine a whole series of fiery forms: a candle flame, glowing coals, fire in a woodstove, an open campfire, a huge bonfire, a grease fire, a burning house after a lightning strike, forest fires, a volcanic eruption with its glowing, destructive lava. Now let's ask ourselves: Which temperament can be hotheaded, is prone to outbursts, accomplishes things with forceful zealousness—and, worst case, erupt like a volcano? The connection to the choleric is obvious! We even use the term "hothead" to describe him and advise him to "keep a cool head."

What about air? Let's look for diverse forms of this element in nature. It is said that a gentle breath "plays" around us. But it can also become a refreshing breeze, then a wind that at first blows lightly, then grows more intense and increasingly violent, stripping leaves from the trees and finally becoming a destructive storm or hurricane.

The air that constantly surrounds us is light and extremely mobile, connecting us with all other beings, carrying the sounds of our voices to other people and making it possible for us to breathe and thus maintain life. It's also interesting that the wind blows quickly past us and doesn't linger, but is somewhere else the next moment.

Among the temperaments there is one that can be compared to a fresh wind on a beautiful sunny day that blows cheerfully around us and delights us. Well? It's the sanguine person who is often referred to as "happy-go-lucky"; who with her great agility and mobility loves to dart from one impression to the next, doesn't linger long in one spot or like to deal with things for any length of time, swirls up a lot of dust and is gone. At parties and celebrations she's like a "breath of fresh air" with her inner lightness; she spreads goodwill and always helps to create a good mood. When sanguine traits are overbearing (we speak in German of a person who is *stürmisch* or "stormy"), we are probably dealing with a combination of sanguine and choleric temperaments. And when meteorologists refer to the weather on a cloudless day as "calm," we could relate this to the sanguine-phlegmatic temperament.

We have already mentioned a few manifestations of the water element; we will now focus on one of them. Let's imagine a quiet lake, so peaceful that its surface looks as smooth as glass, with the trees and distant mountains reflecting in it. A fish surfaces briefly, snaps at an insect and disappears again. But the surface takes a long time to settle: Ripples radiate in all directions, reach the shoreline, return and move off again into the distance—rhythmically and harmoniously—gradually growing weaker until at last quiet returns, and the lake again becomes a mirror. Another characteristic of water is that it forms drops, round shapes, for example in dew. When it flows slowly as a river or stream, meandering, it turns back and forth in large curves. Another type of continuous back-and-forth is also characteristic: Every day enormous amounts of water evaporate, condense into clouds and flow back to earth in the form of life-giving rain. But water can also freeze into ice and exist in a solid state at the earth's poles and in mountain glaciers. In the case of the temperaments, water assumes an intermediate position between air and earth, which is particularly significant.

It shouldn't be difficult to find the corresponding temperament: It's the phlegmatic person, with his peace-loving, serene character, who loves balance. Like a river that flows forever through the same riverbed in its unchanging form, the phlegmatic loves his established habits; and he also has an inclination toward well-rounded bodily forms.

If we take another look at possible combinations of the temperaments, we can recognize and compare them with our observations of water in nature: Its rising movement during evaporation and cloud formation can be seen as a picture of the phlegmatic-sanguine temperament, while ice formation and solidification toward the earth element corresponds more to the phlegmatic-melancholic.

Last but not least, let's look at the element of earth. It finds expression primarily in all possible landforms. We may think of a wide open plain, a hilly landscape, a mountainside or even the extremes of hot and cold: a burning desert and an icy polar region. What landscape in particular might we associate with the melancholic temperament? Let's imagine huge, partially forested mountains: in the background, high snow-capped peaks; in the foreground, enormous cliffs rising up. Here lie the primitive rocks of the earth reminiscent of earlier ages, the solid granite with its great boulders rounded by the water of thousands of years, inviting wanderers to rest. From here one can look out far into the distance, and the earth with all its beauty lies at one's feet.

We can rely on the solid ground under our feet, which the rocks provide us. They're symbolic of strength, heaviness, stillness and longevity. How insecure we feel in contrast if we have to wade through a swamp! Woe betide us if the ground below gives way!

In contrast to this image of the earth element, let's imagine a cave which we enter with a certain degree of hesitation, perhaps even reverence. Here we experience darkness, depth and impenetrability, the mystery of the earth element. But in this darkness the mineralogist can discover rare minerals and the most beautiful sparkling crystals in wonderful shapes and colors!

The melancholic person feels the heaviness and firmness of her body and also likes to withdraw, to retreat within herself— as into a cave. She possesses great inwardness, and of all the temperaments, it's easiest for her to form crystal-clear thoughts and think logically. You can always rely on her. She keeps her promises and remembers what someone else has told, promised, or even done to her: It's not easy for her to forget! She can also adhere to order and thoroughness and loves structure. She is only too familiar with the inner darkness of the earth element and experiences it more intensely than others do, for example when she's sad because she has been disappointed or even deceived.

Can we identify landscapes that correspond to the various temperament combinations? Wherever water and earth come

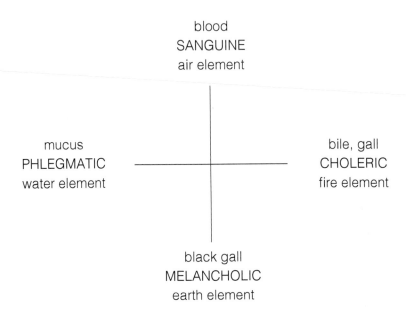

blood
SANGUINE
air element

mucus
PHLEGMATIC
water element

bile, gall
CHOLERIC
fire element

black gall
MELANCHOLIC
earth element

into contact, we can sense the melancholic-phlegmatic character and think of diverse coastal forms, swampy regions or even islands. On the other hand, wherever earth and fire meet, we can expect to find a melancholic-choleric blend and need only think of a landscape at the foot of an active volcano, which is constantly being reformed by the flowing lava and never comes to rest in a final form!

We have the two Greek physicians Hippocrates and Empedocles to thank for the connections between the four temperaments and the four elements that we have tried to picture here. These aspects have been added to the chart above.

The Dangers of Uncontrolled Temperaments

Up to now we have focused on the positive, admirable qualities of each temperament, in order to picture the basic phenomena for further analysis. But we also heard that the physician Hippocrates gained his insights from people who had very little or even no real inner control over their temperaments.

The theory of the temperaments refers to "small and great dangers," and we should keep in mind that the "small" dangers can gradually give way to "great" ones if they are not controlled. This fact can also be imagined as follows: Instead of a person's controlling his temperament and keeping a tight rein on it, as a rider does so that his horse feels it is being guided, he can also be dominated by his temperament so that he loses control of the reins. It's these dangers that we now want to examine.

This time, let's imagine a situation with an intensely *choleric person*, someone who possesses a lot of "inner fire," and let's observe him step by step as he loses his temper. He's about to leave the house and the phone rings. "Stupid telephone!" He's in a hurry as usual, so his inner drive is interrupted by the phone. How can anybody be calling him now?! Idiotic! The choleric starts to tense up: He feels a hot flush coming on; his neck, cheeks and finally his whole head start to redden. He pulls himself together and picks up the receiver, answers – quite brusquely – says right off that he has no time. He asks for the phone number, wants to write it down, but can't find a pen! The redness starts to reach his ears; the anger – his steadily increasing inner fire – begins to overpower him! Swearing and profanity would help him calm down… "Oh, there's a pen! Thank God!" He can heave a sigh of relief! But then the "volcano" erupts: "The damn thing doesn't write, it must be out of ink!!!" He begins to swear, to rant, throws the pen on the floor, steps on it, stamps on "the stupid thing" again and again, insults one of his loved ones who's to blame for all his bad luck (we could compare this with the lava a volcano spews), hurriedly snatches up his briefcase, rushes out of the house and slams the door loudly behind him!

Here we can clearly see how the natural forces of fire are at work in a person if he isn't capable of taming them. But just as every fire goes out when it is no longer fed, every choleric also finally calms down, comes round to his senses and later—in many cases not until the following day—regrets how he's acted. Then he feels the deep need to make up for what he did to his fellow man, for what he's "singed" with his inner fire, although most often he doesn't recall exactly what he said or did.

Already from this example we can see how important it is, in dealing with the temperaments every day, to acquire a basic understanding beforehand so we can deal practically with the diverse temperaments. Since in my opinion it is especially difficult for a "strongly choleric" person to manage social situations and be understood, I've dealt with him in a bit more detail.

The minor danger of this temperament we could refer to as irritability, or the inclination to get angry. The larger danger would be "rage" or "raving madness," but outbursts of anger or temper also fall in this category when someone is seething or truly furious.

Many people might experience an isolated outburst of anger independent of their temperament, and this alone will not mark someone as a choleric. It's only when the angry outbursts grow frequent and finally habitual that a person could be considered "easily angered." In this example all the stages were depicted, from emotional indignation to a habitual outbreak of anger and finally a fit of rage.

In the case of a *phlegmatic person* the description is much easier. Let's first empathize and experience her wonderful quality of calmness and composure. Now let's try to feel what it's like to let ourselves become impassive: We respond to impressions from outside as if they interested us less and less. So the possibility definitely exists that when her impassivity begins to take more and more control of her, our phlegmatic person will grow noticeably less open to the world around her and increasingly uninterested in life.

If she then increases this disinterest even further, she loses interest in embracing what's happening around her with her senses, and they become weaker and weaker. Feeble-mindedness, dulling of the senses and apathy are the result. But because at least one interest—the pleasure of the palate—always remains, and in most cases even increases, it often happens that the body expands as well. This in turn leads to her disinterest and apathy increasing even more! A therapist with a lot of experience working with such cases pointed out to me that she can help them only if she is able to discover something they are still genuinely interested in. She reports that, unfortunately, there are people who no longer evince even the slightest spark of interest. In such cases all that remains is the joy of eating—substantial quantities.

To summarize: Disinterest and imbecility are the hazards of the phlegmatic temperament.

Next, let's imagine that a *sanguine person*—borne by the air element—shows interest in everything around him, is open to the whole world, lovingly carries out his role in the community, etc. But if he becomes "breezier" and more "air-headed," his temperament can begin to slip out of his grasp. His interests change too fast; he's constantly looking for new impressions; he's less absorbed in matters; he's unable to pay attention to anything for a long time; he likes to start new things without completing them and has a hard time achieving peace and quiet.

In brief, he becomes "flighty." What he'd like most is to flit like a butterfly from one flower to another, sipping the sweet nectar. If his temperament takes an even stronger hold on him, he becomes even more restless, and crazy ideas and deeds can result. Finally he may lose his inner stability, unless he has someone at his side who understands how to lovingly "ground" him and guide him back to the realities of life.

To summarize: Flightiness and insanity are the two possible extremes of this temperament.

Let's now slip into the skin of a *melancholic person* who thinks seriously about herself and the world around her, feels empathy with others and, in contrast to the sanguine, possesses much inwardness. If she begins to concentrate too much on herself, takes everything personally, criticizes constantly and becomes more and more pessimistic, she will begin to suffer from her gloominess—the "small" hazard of this temperament—and to withdraw into herself. In this state she can become moody and complain about all the things in her surroundings that have always bothered her. A state of mind like this can grow more and more intense and ultimately result in her becoming miserably despondent.

Gloominess and despondency are the two hazards of the melancholic temperament.

Temperament	minor danger	major danger
Choleric person	irritability	rage
Phlegmatic person	lack of interest	imbecility
Sanguine person	flightiness	insanity
Melancholic person	gloominess	despondency

Readers already familiar with the subject of this book will have noticed that the "minor dangers" highlighted here are actually all the interesting quirks and obvious traits we normally associate with the temperaments and which are well known. It's easy to see why the extreme forms of the temperaments have supplied comedians, artists and authors with ample material to lampoon— it can be outrageously funny to see our (and other people's) exaggerated qualities mirrored, and it lets us have a good laugh.

In summary, we can say that the magnificent manifestations of the temperaments are not only individually colored in every person, but also produce a rich range of colors depending on the degree to which each individual has mastered them. This is what makes the temperaments so varied, interesting and appealing!

With all that we have learned from the descriptions of temperaments in children and from some basic concepts of temperament theory, we now want to focus on the adult world with its multi-colored hues produced by the temperaments. A good way to start is by contemplating the "temperament rose" produced by Goethe and Schiller.

The "Temperament Rose" of Goethe and Schiller

The two great German poets and close friends, Johann Wolfgang von Goethe and Friedrich Schiller, were presumably in a good mood when they took a closer look at the various combinations of the temperaments and arrived at a total of twelve different aspects. They also identified twelve corresponding colors, which are not given here because their connection to the temperaments is not particularly easy to comprehend. (In a later chapter we will, however, be able to find a connection to four colors.)

First of all, we can see that the melancholic temperament was put at the top and the sanguine at the bottom. Now let's try to understand how the two poets arrived at the interesting terms they chose.

Their assigning of the *heroic* quality to the choleric is logical. Qualities such as determination and drive are compatible with this. When a bit of the sanguine temperament is present, the choleric person becomes an *adventurer*. This enables him to react spontaneously with greater flexibility as he moves toward his goal and to confront unexpected situations cheerfully.

We've already become acquainted with the sanguine person as someone who is open to the world around her and interested in many things, especially other people. Hand in hand with this comes a great capacity to love: She is the *lover*. If a bit of choleric temperament—the determined orientation toward a goal—combines with the sanguine, the enjoyment of pleasure becomes a goal and is more consciously pursued: The person becomes a *bon vivant* who knows how to make the best of life.

The poets imagined the phlegmatic as the ideal *historian*. After all, if we occupy ourselves with the past, we won't experience anything too agitating—we can just describe it calmly, and

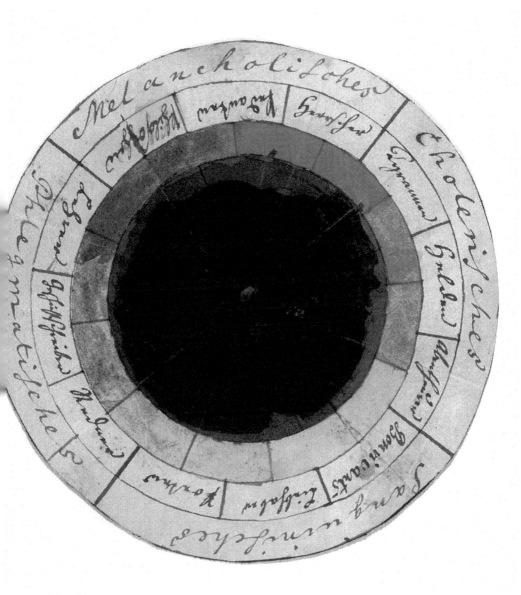

The "Temperament Rose" of Goethe and Schiller (1809).
Watercolor from 1799.

Diagram of the "temperament rose," combined with Goethe's symmetrical color wheel of 1809.

while we're writing, we don't even need to talk! If a bit of the sanguine temperament mixes in, the phlegmatic person becomes a *speaker* or *orator*. The airy element creates slight waves on the surface of the otherwise peacefully flowing current. (I once had a phlegmatic-sanguine student who could hardly be stopped when he started to inundate his neighbor with a torrent of words. Once, while telling a story to the class, I asked him if he would please stop talking. He said yes, and I continued with my story—and he continued with his. I asked him again; he nodded in reply, stopped briefly, then started again. When I asked why he had kept on talking despite his promise, he pleasantly replied: "I wasn't finished yet.") The imaginative and eloquent sanguine person becomes the *poet* when his temperament mixes with the watery rhythms and waves of the phlegmatic temperament.

Goethe and Schiller saw the melancholic as a *dogmatist*, a *pedant*, by which they meant one who loves order and takes things very seriously and precisely—two very valuable qualities. Further aspects of this temperament are earnestness, a strong intellectual capacity and the ability to empathize deeply. When choleric characteristics such as determination and drive mix with the melancholic temperament, one positive result is leadership qualities. The person becomes a *ruler*—today we might also say a "boss"—a role for which the sanguine person is less suited, because she loves all her employees and always tries to please everyone. In the combination of the choleric and melancholic temperaments, Goethe and Schiller also saw the possibility of becoming a *tyrant*. Whoever has had dealings with such people will be able to confirm this.

If the melancholic mixes with the phlegmatic—the water element—thought processes begin to flow, and the person becomes a *philosopher*. The calm, peace-loving phlegmatic becomes a *teacher* when the serious intellectual nuances of the melancholic temperament mix in. In Goethe and Schiller's day this might have been the appropriate combination. But Rudolf Steiner urged his teachers to harmonize all four temperaments in themselves and learn to master them to such a degree that they could become sanguine with the sanguine child, choleric (but self-controlled, without anger) with the choleric child, and so on with the other two temperaments.

The temperament rose can be very helpful for visualizing these combinations. If we recall that a tendency toward every temperament exists in each one of us, we shouldn't be surprised if, in certain situations, we see a person react completely differently from what we would expect, so that a designation from another area of the rose would seem more appropriate.

Goethe and Schiller ingeniously and intuitively arrived at their twelve designations without including the basic concepts that we have been developing. But we'll keep looking for a way to slip into the temperaments and understand them from the inside.

4. A Deeper Comprehension of the Temperaments

How to Understand a Temperament

Let's use a sanguine person to try to demonstrate how we can achieve a deeper understanding of a temperament. The physician Hippocrates, who used homeopathy to treat illness, coined an interesting phrase to summarize his approach: Things that are similar identify with each other; things that are similar cure each other, or, put more simply, "Like cures like."

It's the first part of this formula that we'll be dealing with, since a temperament cannot be characterized as an illness. If we want to slip into a sanguine person and feel what she feels, we need to become sanguine ourselves. Depending on our own temperament, becoming appropriately agile and quick will be quite easy for some, harder for others. The following exercise can be helpful. We can try to occupy and associate ourselves inwardly with all possible aspects of the air element so that our thought processes become more and more lively and adaptable, and through this inner activity we will simultaneously learn, so to speak, to feel "airy."

As we immerse ourselves into the air element we try, like air, to expand as far as possible, to penetrate into every opening, to move quickly. We touch things gently, barely stroking their surface; we are imbued with light, blow quickly, nimbly, dynamically up and down, back and forth, emanate and breathe out and breathe in again, like the great breath of all living things. We don't like to be compressed or confined; we're interested in everything around us, discover every hiding place, every nook and cranny; we unite all living things, won't let ourselves be caught, play games with people's hats, and much more. After all, we know all the nuances from calm to storm and can easily transform ourselves into everything in between.

If we are able to feel "airy" this way, we get closer to the sanguine person, slip into the essence of the temperament, experience it from inside and understand it! We notice that we exert quite a lot of energy and activity to achieve this result. And slipping into the other three temperaments similarly requires an enlivening inner experience of their respective characteristics. The characteristics described earlier and in what follows can provide you with the basics to help with your own efforts.

The methods developed in this chapter can also serve as a basis for imaginatively picturing situations in the lives of adults. We can slip into all four elements and imagine the experiences of four fictional persons who are surprised by something unexpected. The creative imagination we need to develop can be described by Goethe's term "exact fantasy": The characteristics of the individual elements are the guiding principle for our imaginative process, so we don't get sidetracked and deviate into the realm of the "fantastical."

In an Elevator

Let's imagine that four people with different temperaments meet in an elevator. What might their reactions be when the elevator suddenly gets stuck?

The choleric reacts indignantly, since she has a meeting scheduled, a goal! "This technology! It's all good for nothing! We've got to do something!" Over to the control panel at once! Press the red button: Emergency! Alarm! Talk into the intercom! It doesn't work! That's typical! Wait for help? Are you kidding? Pound on the door, call for help! "All together on the count of three!"... "Nothing but trouble wherever you go!" This waiting is unbearable... To herself: It's unbelievable that nobody else is doing anything! Weird people! Of course I've got to do everything on my own again! – All we do is wait! This is unbearable! ... "Ah, it's working again! Well, finally! I guess the intercom did work after all! Typical! I should have known! Stupid elevator! ... Bye!"

How differently the phlegmatic person reacts. He smiles quietly to himself: "OK, I guess I'll be getting to work late... that's not so bad, it's not my fault." To the others: "Now just don't panic

… stay calm. I'm sure help will come soon." He unhurriedly takes out his lunchbox and says to himself: "Time for my morning snack. How great that nobody's here to remind me to get back to work!" He makes himself comfortable … he'd really love to be able to sit down … watches calmly as the choleric lady springs into action for the rest of them, and thinks: "Wow, she's making quite a ruckus! She's one of those people who's always in a hurry … just like my boss – (later): Oh well, the elevator's moving again … Too bad, I'm not even done with my snack yet. So long!"

The door is already half closed when the sanguine squeezes into the elevator, takes a quick look around in all directions, and with a friendly twinkle in her eye greets everyone cheerfully, as if they were all old friends. Another quick glimpse and she's decided who looks really good and what everybody is wearing. "Ha, the elevator's stuck; that takes the cake – today I'll be getting in late!" – To the others: "Are you all in a hurry? I'm not. May I introduce myself? My name is Toni Schulz. I work on the fourth floor. What about you? What a nice opportunity to meet you – I guess bad luck can have its good side!" (To the choleric lady): "It's really nice of you to take charge. But don't get too upset – as I always say, being angry isn't good for you, haha!" (To the others): "Actually, it's really a great day today: What beautiful weather! Much too nice to spend sitting around at the office; I'd rather be sailing; have you got a hobby, too? – no? But everyone should have a hobby; I have a lot of them, I love to go…oh, the elevator's working again. Wow, that went really fast; it was nice meeting you all; maybe we'll meet again soon; I really hope so; all the best and have a great day!"

The melancholic person—serious, sober, with head bowed—enters the narrow confines of the elevator, which he dislikes anyway. He quietly and attentively observes the others, begins to wonder about them; then the sanguine woman greets him in such a friendly way that he has no choice but to respond. He retreats again into his thoughts and says to himself: "No, there's no way I would approach other people like that – you just don't do that, they're complete strangers; you don't know them at all ... She is nice, I must admit that, but a bit too forward – she acts like we're old friends." Oh my goodness, isn't the elevator working? With inner dismay: "Why does this have to happen to me too? Isn't it terrible? What do we do now? ... Didn't I have a premonition this morning when I woke up? I should have listened to my inner voice – but now it's too late ... (He observes the choleric woman:) Thank God she's making such a racket – normally this much noise would bother me, but now it's the right thing to do, probably the only thing that can save us ... I wonder if she's always like this? ... Now she wants all of us to start yelling. That's not going to help, either ... What's my boss going to say? He's probably already wondering where I am. He knows I'm always punctual. – Oh, what a relief! ... it's working again ... we're saved!" – (To the choleric): "How lucky for us that you were here! Thank you so much, I'll never forget what you did ... Goodbye!"

Some Graphic Examples

Pictures often speak louder than words to show how the temperaments react in certain situations. Two examples will illustrate how our topic can be shown graphically: "A Rock Blocking the Path" and "The Hat on the Park Bench." On the following pages we see the reactions of the different temperaments depicted humorously.

A Rock Blocking the Path

The choleric immediately and forcefully removes the obstacle in his path.

The phlegmatic sits down on the rock and makes himself comfortable.

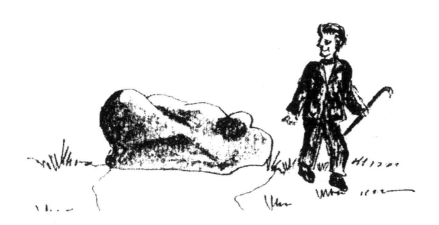

The melancholic is concerned and steers clear of the obstacle. Or he sits down on it and asks himself: "Why did this have to happen to *me*?"

The sanguine jumps merrily over the obstacle.

The Hat on the Park Bench

The choleric gets angry and scolds the wrongdoer.

The phlegmatic remains calm and puts the squashed hat back on.

The melancholic is shocked and begins to despair.

The sanguine thinks it's funny and laughs heartily about it.

Further Exercises for Comprehending the Temperaments

As we did in the elevator example, the interested reader could look at any number of additional situations and try to paint his or her own inner pictures of what might happen by using the "exact fantasy" method. The following situations lend themselves to this particularly well, if we begin with the question: How do the temperaments act

- when they get up in the morning and go to work?
- when they've overslept?
- when they have to wait a long time for the bus?
- when they get to work too late?
- when the phone rings at an inconvenient time?
- when they get stuck in a traffic jam on the expressway and have to wait?
- when a homemaker would like a break from housework and the children start to cry?
- when all four of them meet at a restaurant?
- when they work as a salesperson or at the post office or ticket office?
- when they party together?

... and many more situations that readers will be able to imagine.

The two examples in the illustrations on the previous pages make it clear that a good sense of humor is important when imagining these situations. It can also be interesting to act them out in a group. This usually leads to a lot of laughs, but at the same time it sharpens the observer's awareness of characteristic aspects and reactions.

The more actively we practice these exercises, the more adept we'll become at imagining them, learning how to slip into them, and recognizing them from many different angles. If we return our attention to children, exercises like these can be quite useful—apart from acting out scenes together.

Here's a list of everyday situations with children that are worth imagining in the four characteristic ways:
- how they get up and get dressed in the morning
- how they act when their parents have overslept and everyone's late
- how they come into the kitchen to see what's for dinner
- how they sit at the table and eat
- how and when they tackle their homework
- how they play
- how they cultivate friendships
- whether and how they help around the house
- how they act when they're put to bed
- how they react when their parents are expecting company in the evening and when the guests arrive

When doing this it's important to note that it can of course be initially helpful to picture what you've personally experienced with your own or other children. But to a certain extent you should free yourself from such preconceptions so you can fully immerse yourself in the creative imagination process. This will be more successful if you don't focus on a particular child.

There's another exercise that can be recommended for further practice. Using colored chalk or crayons, try to draw like a child in the style of all four temperaments. How would a sanguine or choleric child draw a house, for example, with a tree next to it, or a meadow with a child or animal? A sanguine child's tree might be freely and loosely rooted in the ground, with thin, airy branches on top; a choleric child's drawing would probably be much more forceful in form and color! In this way both your inner and outer eyes for the temperaments can be developed further.

Rudolf Steiner's Diagram for Recognizing the Temperaments

In his course for teachers,[3] Rudolf Steiner drew an interesting diagram on the blackboard to help all those trying to identify a student's predominant temperament. The diagram asks us to adopt two different points of view.

First, we can ask ourselves what temperaments strongly react to sense impressions and are easily stimulated from the outside, or, as Steiner puts it, how "excitable" are they? If we recall everything we've learned so far, it should be obvious that this is characteristic of the sanguines and cholerics. Here's an example from my own experience: I was teaching in one of the lower grades whose classroom was located at ground level. Through the big windows you could see a long, high hedge. Suddenly a little red squirrel sprang from branch to branch along the whole length of the hedge. The children were delighted and some of them jumped up from their desks and ran to the window. Which ones were they? The melancholic children were engrossed in the lesson and didn't notice anything until the first children sprang up from their seats; they remained seated because they remembered that the teacher had said you shouldn't run around in class. The phlegmatic children also daydreamed through the incident; getting up wasn't really worth the effort because they weren't overly interested, having already seen such animals many times.

Secondly, we can ask: With how much inner strength do the temperaments respond to and identify with such impressions from outside? Here, too, there are two temperaments that do this well: choleric and melancholic. The fact that the choleric pursues the goal he has set for himself with perseverance and determination to the very end shows his great inner strength. And it's not uncommon for a choleric person also to possess physical strength! In the case of a melancholic, we know she identifies with things closely and intensively and can devote herself to them with perseverance and, in particular, painstaking thoroughness; this evidences her great inner strength.

Now we can understand from a different perspective why the sanguine fellow has so little staying power and loves rapid change: The joy and pleasure he gets from new impressions is intense, but because of his "low strength" he can't identify with and respond to them strongly enough. In a phlegmatic person we can recognize "low strength" as well as "low excitability" from the fact that she doesn't like to change conditions in which she feels comfortable; she prefers to maintain them.

If we look at the diagram based on Rudolf Steiner's indications, we can clearly see that this, too, results in a four-part division of characteristics, answering the frequently heard question: Why are there only four possibilities—and not, for instance, five or eleven?

This diagram can be an invaluable help in dealing with children or adults if, over a period of time, we observe exactly and learn to answer correctly the questions about a person's "excitability" and "inner strength." It goes without saying that this shouldn't be a snap judgment; constant observation and inner questioning are necessary if we want to do justice to the person whose temperament we are trying to determine.

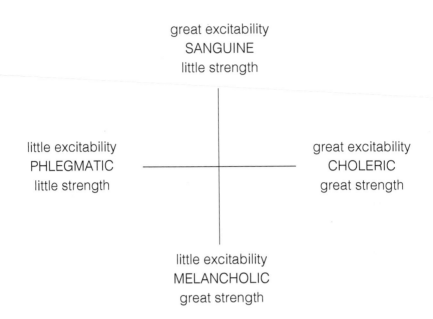

Hidden Characteristics of the Temperaments

Even if we have known another person for a long time and think we know her well, including identifying her main temperament, we will nevertheless be in for a few surprises now and then. We will notice that in some of her habits, the person reacts completely differently than we would expect based on her temperament, and even according to the combination of her two predominant temperaments. So we might think, "That's not like her, it's not at all in keeping with her temperament."

But thank goodness that this does happen! It would hardly be bearable for those around him if someone we considered choleric reacted cholerically in all life situations, if from the moment he got up—brushing his teeth, showering, drying himself off, having breakfast, reading the paper—and in all other activities during the day he were always "full steam ahead" at top volume! If we look closely, we'll discover that in everybody's case there are little habits here and there that reveal their less obvious, more obscure temperaments. After all, we did say that each of us has all four, so we should be able to discover them!

When searching for such hidden aspects, I discovered about myself, for example, that while I am sanguine and choleric in many respects, I really let my phlegmatic side show when it comes to supper: I can eat the same things over and over again, be it summer or winter, weekday, weekend or holiday! I also always eat my food in the same order. But the fact that this is a typical phlegmatic gesture didn't dawn on me until recently. My hidden melancholic side is also rarely noticed by others. It appears when I begin to brood over things that didn't go as well as I had hoped and that I can't change. My wife, who's more strongly blessed with a melancholic temperament, is particularly sanguine when it comes to supper. She likes variety in the foods she eats, switches them often and always has new ideas about what she'd like to try.

It's really fascinating to hear different people describe the situations and habits in which their more hidden temperaments reveal themselves. Here are a few more examples:

A mother told me that her daughter never experiences her as angry at home, and that she possesses hardly any choleric characteristics and is always able to remain calm and composed... except for one situation that can hit her like a bolt out of the blue and make her fly into a rage—to her daughter's horror. She can't bear it when she's on the street and sees a dog that doesn't obey; when there's a dog at an intersection or on the curb that doesn't immediately sit when its owner tells it to, she can hit the roof and—if the situation allows it—give the owner a piece of her mind. There's no other situation in which her choleric side reveals itself! This kind of "thunderstorm" breaks out only in those situations, and she always reacts the same way—habitually. And reacting according to one's temperament, of course, means the same as reacting out of habit.

A father I've known for a long time and admire very much because of his strong choleric drive and determination, as well as his pronounced melancholic characteristics of seriousness and thoroughness, once told me about an interesting leisure activity of his, an activity which reveals his hidden phlegmatic side: He has a hunting license and every once in a while he just loves to go out at night to sit in his blind, motionless for hours, waiting and waiting ... enjoying the peace and quiet. In addition, his friends all describe him as a gourmet.

In a seminar with adult students we examined the participants' less obvious temperaments and made some interesting discoveries. They agreed to let me mention a few here:

An older participant, the mother of several children who is predominantly phlegmatic and melancholic, can also sometimes get very irritated and clearly express her anger. When I asked her where her sanguine side was, she spontaneously responded: Whenever she is near a large body of water, a pond, lake, river or sea, and sees the wind blowing across the surface, she suddenly feels light and vivacious, wants to hop, skip and laugh and joyfully hug the whole world. And the feeling doesn't go away quickly—it lasts a while!

Another student realized that, although he is otherwise very melancholic/phlegmatic, he always spontaneously reacts cholerically and vehemently when a dog gets near him. And he almost always also gets barked at. His girlfriend, who was convinced her temperament was very similar to his, was sure she had absolutely no choleric tendencies. It was priceless when he reminded her how intensely she often swears when driving—at other drivers who aren't driving carefully enough!

A female student with primarily sanguine traits suddenly discovered her melancholic side: She loved it when other people came to her to discuss their personal problems—especially at great length.

A hairdresser, happy that thanks to her sanguine temperament she was always able to get interested in talking to her next customer, discovered her hidden phlegmatic and melancholic sides just a few moments after I posed the question: While the rest of her family loves to watch sports on TV, she has absolutely no interest in it and instead enjoys cuddling up in a comfortable armchair to read, read, read...

These few examples show us that there are subtler qualities in each person that we can discover only over time. Since they have to do with recurring habits, we can correctly assume that we are dealing with one or two temperaments that aren't readily recognizable.

Up to now our discussion of the temperaments has barely touched upon their more hidden aspects. So for those who consider the identification of temperaments to be merely a system of labeling or classification, this aspect can offer a new way of approaching the idea of temperaments more openly and without reservations. By using the above methods of observation, we always focus on the person as a whole; and we can rest assured that we will take quite a long time to fully recognize ourselves and others in every small, subtle nuance and detail.

5. A Closer Look at the Human Being

Understanding the "Four Parts of Being"

Before we go on to discuss how to deal with the temperaments practically and pedagogically, let's first briefly define some terms that are necessary to widen our perspective, and then return to our topic. Let's attempt, as objectively as possible, to compare the human being with the three other kingdoms of nature: the mineral, plant and animal realms. What do we have in common with each of them?

From the point of view of the mineral realm, we can identify our physical bodies, which are composed of matter, the same substances that are found in the earth, in minerals. If we think of all the elements in the periodic table, it's amazing to learn that we can find the faintest traces of nearly every one of them in our body.

This body is subject to the laws of gravity, and during our lives we must continually expend energy to stand erect and to move. We mentioned this fact when we looked at the four elements and referred to the earth element.

When we die, our physical body cannot maintain its form and already begins to decompose after a few moments, and this decomposition goes on and on. We also know that after several years the body disintegrates completely and turns back into earth. So during one's whole life, there must be some force present that is responsible for keeping the physical body from decomposing.

Before we take the next step, let's look for a moment at the plant realm and compare it with what we've determined about the mineral realm. We can ask ourselves: What fundamental abilities does a plant have which we do not find in a mineral?

We'll discover that plants have the natural, inborn ability to *grow*. After blossoming they produce fruit and seeds, so they are able to *reproduce*. From mowing the lawn we know all too well that the grass will grow back, that plants have an ability that we call *regeneration*. If we ask ourselves which of the four temperaments the plant has a particularly strong connection to, it quickly becomes clear that it always needs enough moisture, enough water. If we don't give it enough water, it will die. And that in turn means that it is a living creation. We also find this force that maintains life in animals and in people, along with the capacities for growth, reproduction and regeneration. In contrast, the mineral is not alive in this sense. It doesn't die and it doesn't reproduce.

This life force that we encounter in plant, animal and human permeates the physical body and keeps it alive. By doing so, it constantly prevents its decomposition. Rudolf Steiner called the organism of these life forces the "life body" or "etheric body." He uses the term *body* because the life forces flowing through us appear, to those capable of perceiving it, in the form of an invisible formation or structure of energy. Each plant, for example, has its own life force which, when it wilts in autumn, remains bonded to the seed and brings forth the plant form anew the following year.

In the case of the human being, these life forces are also closely connected with all that is liquid in us, which is involved in the metabolic and growth processes in the body. Rudolf Steiner also used the graphic term "the architect within us" to refer to the "life body" because it bears and preserves our individual blueprints and is capable of completely healing a wound: an interesting example of regeneration.

Let's now look at the animal realm and ask ourselves: What fundamental abilities does an animal have that a plant does not? We discover that an animal can seek its food out of its own *initiative* and instinctively *move* to where it can find it. A plant does not yet possess the ability to move. The fact that in the course of a day many plants continuously turn their blossoms to face the sun, and therefore do move in a sense (a form of heliotropism), is not the same as the animal's spatial movement to seek food.

In contrast to a plant, an animal possesses an inner faculty for *sense perception*, connected to the fact that it has sense organs with which it perceives the world. Whatever it perceives with its senses becomes inner experience by way of its sensations. Many animals, for example, have a strong perception of smells; others of a certain taste. In dogs, the sense of smell is particularly well developed: They have to smell everything and actually follow their noses when they run so they can sniff everything imaginable. Cats, with their well-developed sense of sight, have more intense sensations connected with vision.

Compared to a plant, we recognize that an animal has a *soul* through which it can feel inside but also relate to the world around it. Rudolf Steiner calls this soul concept, which also reveals itself like a bodily form, the "soul body" or "astral body." Humans also possess such a body. In a human being diverse drives, impulses, desires and emotions also exist, and by means of this soul body we can experience joy, suffering, pain. Our ability to feel and to perceive with our senses is closely connected with our breathing processes and therefore with the air element. Just as we inhale and exhale air, we can turn our attention by means of our soul to focus alternately outward for a while and then inward again.

Finally, what fundamental abilities does the human being possess that we don't find in an animal? We are beings extremely capable of learning, who from the very outset depend on human examples to be able to develop basic abilities. These include *standing upright, walking, speaking* and *thinking.* Children who were abandoned and raised by animals such as wolves, foxes or bears learned to crawl on all fours and, after being returned to human care, learned to stand only partially erect—which is the prerequisite for being able to learn to walk, speak and think by means of imitation and trial and error. Most of these children learned to walk, but only a few developed speech, and none of them developed the ability to think clearly.

Up to the second or third year of life, young children use their own first names to refer to themselves, but then suddenly, from one day to the next, they acquire a first consciousness of themselves and feel themselves to be an ego, an "I." This *consciousness of self* is a characteristic trait of human beings that cannot be observed in the case of animals. Only a few of the abandoned children were able to acquire this self-awareness, and the fact that none of them survived longer than nine years shows us that the fundamental abilities described are essential for a life that is fit for human beings. These three abilities which belong to the ego or "I"—upright carriage, speech and a consciousness of self that is capable of thought—are not present in an animal.

So there exists a spiritual force that maintains and is characteristic only of the human being. Every human being refers to him- or herself as "I." As a physical-spiritual being, each human being also has an ego that differentiates him or her from every other person. This ego develops in the course of a lifetime, enriched by life experiences. Already from the moment of birth, the ego-force is active within us: It raises us upright in the first year of life, helps us to our feet and leads us step by step into life. It shines out of the bright eyes of a child when she stands up for the first time.

As with the other aspects of our being, if we take a look at the element that enables our ego to work within our body, it is the warmth (the element of fire) that flows through us. When we have a fever, we experience that this warmth can rise in temperature; in cases of frostbite and freezing, we experience that our inner warmth was not sufficient to withstand the cold forcing itself in. Our ego imperceptibly regulates our constant inner temperature.

In conclusion we can say: Every person consists of the four different parts outlined here. Rudolf Steiner referred to them as the "members" or "parts of being" in terms that we will use, namely the ego, the soul or astral body, the life or etheric body and the physical body.

The effects of the four members of our being can be observed through the four elements in the realms of nature and also in humans, so that we can conclude the following: As a result of the fact that a human being is the carrier of an ego and at the same time is sustained by it, the ego can transform the three other members of our being.

In order to understand this, let's look again at a plant: Aside from its physical body, it has a life body. This produces the most diverse forms of plant life, depending on the species, so we can conclude that different plants, flowers and trees are a physical image of the invisible life forces at work within them.

When observing the animal, we recognize the soul or astral body, which is less highly differentiated in lower animal species but very differentiated in higher ones. It influences the animal's etheric body and redesigns it, and many diverse physical animal forms are brought forth with its help. So we can say that an individual animal species is the image of the invisible astral forces that are at work within it.

In the human being, the power and ability to change lie deeply within us. The ego first influences the astral or soul body, transforms it and redesigns the life or etheric body with its help. This ultimately leads to a reorganization or transformation of the physical body, so we can say that our physical body is also an expression of the ego forces within us. Our ego permeates all the members of our being, and over the course of our lives, it is also capable of changing itself, further developing and even teaching itself.

Let's take a look at a very interesting expression that we rarely think about. What does it really mean when we say, "I teach (or educate) myself"? Doesn't this suggest that there are actually two of us—one that educates and knows how to teach, and one that is to be educated? In both cases we're talking about an ego. The educator ego must be greater, wiser and more significant if it has mastered the ability to teach or educate, and it must be conscious of the aims and objectives of the other ego. Rudolf Steiner calls this the "higher ego" or the "eternal individuality" that exists in every human being. It is a spiritual entity within us whose existence we sense, which represents something eternal within us, stays united with us from one lifetime to the next and constantly strives to improve itself. In contrast we can simply refer to the other as the "I" or "ego." And this is what we will be referring to when we look again at the temperaments and see them in connection with what we have explored so far in this chapter.

The "Parts of Being" and the Temperaments

In order to imagine the "parts of being" at work within us, we can again compare the kingdoms of nature with the human being. And in order to understand the temperaments, we no longer need to look at their connection with mineral, plant and animal, but rather with the four elements. Let's take a look at them in the following list:

Parts of Being	Elements
ego/the "I"	warmth
soul or astral body	air
life or etheric body	water
physical body	earth

It should not be too difficult to relate the temperaments to the four parts of being, since we've already taken a close look at their connection with the elements. Nevertheless, there are several new aspects to consider which will give us deeper insight into our topic.

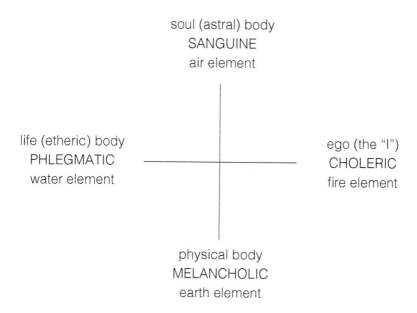

soul (astral) body
SANGUINE
air element

life (etheric) body
PHLEGMATIC
water element

ego (the "I")
CHOLERIC
fire element

physical body
MELANCHOLIC
earth element

Let's begin with the melancholic personality: He experiences the heaviness of his physical body and also has a hard time keeping it sufficiently warm. This physical entity also has solid substance inside it, and in comparison with the other parts of being, darkness or absence of light reigns within it. The melancholic can sense this solidity and absence of light within his soul qualities, and feels affected and restricted by them.

In the case of the phlegmatic personality, it is the life or etheric body together with the water element that lend composure and equilibrium. The forces of the etheric body give rise to the peaceful flow of the lymphatic and other processes that permeate us and have a regenerative function in nutrition, in digestion, in metabolism. Knowing this, we can more easily understand the fact that the phlegmatic person derives special pleasure from eating and drinking.

The sanguine personality's enjoyment of rapidly changing sense impressions also becomes understandable when we learn that it is our soul or astral body that conveys all the emotions we experience. In connection with our breathing—and thus with the air element—it is an extremely agile part of our being. In earlier times, the air element was seen in close connection with light. We see this connection reaffirmed when we hear that the astral body is connected with our thought processes, which help us "shed light" on so many things. Thus we say, "It dawned on me," when we understand something with the help of our thinking. The sanguine personality with his sunny nature can radiate a lot of brightness, though he seldom uses it to think anything through thoroughly.

The fact that the fire element characterizes the choleric temperament has been examined already. Now let's move on from the ego to the "higher ego" in this connection. With her ego a choleric person exerts her willpower to achieve her goals, and this is her source of determination and drive. Her willpower is the fiery energy with which she removes obstacles from her way. If resistance is too great, the ego reacts and fights against it, intensifies its inner fire, forces the heat upward into the head and robs the person of her ability to think clearly. Once this point is reached, the ego does an about-face and then must finally seek release in the form of involuntary movements of the arms or legs. When the ego is finally able to calm itself down, the excessive heat of excitement decreases, and the head slowly returns to being an organ of perception and thought.

From this study we can see that together with the corresponding elements, the parts of our being are the actual basis for the temperaments. These parts are developed to a different degree in each of us. The most dominant part of our being determines which temperament will appear most clearly, but here, too, we see that all four are always present and should be perceptible to us. At the same time we recognize that the parts of our being, which work within us as a spiritual force, correspond to the elements that serve as their physical foundation and thus represent a part of "nature" within us. If this nature becomes too dominant, our temperament takes over: As an example of this, we've already compared a particularly excitable, hotheaded choleric person to a volcano. When a volcano erupts in nature, we accept this as a natural occurrence. And when a choleric person explodes in anger, we should also consider this, to a certain degree, a natural occurrence and learn to react accordingly.

It's our task to keep nature within us in harmony, in balance, so we are not overpowered or ruled by it. And to achieve this we require not only appropriate exercises (see pages 215–219), but strong spiritual powers that we can acquire through self-control and self-teaching. We can rightfully say that by working on the temperaments, we should be able to bring our parts of being into balance and greater harmony, to make them function better together.

Temperament is something within us that is universally human. Each of us has it in some form inside us. If it expresses itself too strongly and dominates us, it becomes our task to work on harmonizing it. Our individual nature leaves its mark on our predisposition to the temperaments, so that no one else can be just like us.

But we can still ask ourselves this: Why does this or that temperament in particular, or combination of temperaments, appear especially dominant? Is heredity responsible, or perhaps even how we are raised?

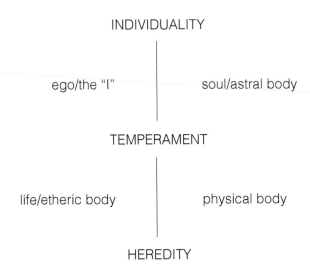

INDIVIDUALITY

ego/the "I"   soul/astral body

TEMPERAMENT

life/etheric body   physical body

HEREDITY

If one's temperament were inherited from one's parents, all the children in a big family would have the same temperament. But just the opposite is more often the case: We usually find all the temperaments and their combinations represented there! For the same reason, upbringing can't be the cause: Siblings develop much too differently for this to be the case.

Rudolf Steiner provides us with an idea that suggests a solution to this puzzling question: Already before birth, the eternal individuality causes the ego and the soul body to unite with all that is given and entrusted to us by our parents through heredity. And what is it that we inherit from our parents? The physical body, the life or etheric body and some of their emotional qualities. All the rest is we ourselves, our own unique personality with our own spiritual and mental abilities!

It's easy to imagine that these spiritual and mental powers are not easily brought into harmony with what we inherit. For the most diverse powers must be able to permeate each other: The most individual essence of our being encounters what is offered to us by our parents and has to unite and harmonize with it. The word *temperament* means "mixture," so we can therefore say that our main temperament more or less represents the net result of these different forces within us. We can also compare this process to that of a painter who has the primary colors on a palette and uses them to mix completely new, unexpected shades before applying them to the canvas and creating a picture.

We have already said: No human being can be exactly like any other, not even when both have the same main temperament. Now we can understand why: Our individuality with its powers takes hold of our hereditary stream, colors it in its own way, and the resulting mixture is what we term our temperament.

So our temperament takes shape in the middle, between the very own impulses our individuality brings with it into life and what comes from heredity. So it is we ourselves who wish to master this lifetime with this particular, individually colored shade of temperament. We would do someone a great injustice if we harbored thoughts or expressed the opinion that in her case it's unfortunate that a certain temperament is so dominant. This would be nothing more than a violation of her personal freedom.

One's temperament does not constitute the entire human being! If we are aware of someone's temperament, we are a long way from completely grasping and comprehending her real personality, her individuality. The parts of her being that we become familiar with in connection with the temperaments are comparable only to the "clothes" or outer layers in which her individuality is active. But it's through these overlays and the temperaments that we can begin to sense and understand the mystery of her individuality, if we do this with a deep sense of emotion: with love.

At the end of a lecture about the mystery of the temperaments, Rudolf Steiner said the following: "We learn to know the individual human being in every respect when we perceive him in the light of spiritual science. We learn to perceive even the child this way. We learn little by little to respect, to value in the child the peculiarity, the enigmatic quality of the individuality, and we learn also how we must treat this individual in life because spiritual science gives us not merely general, theoretical directions. It guides us in our relation to the individual in the solving of the riddles that are there to be solved.

"These solutions are to love him as we must love him if we do not merely fathom him with the mind. We must let him work upon us completely. We must let our spiritual scientific insight give wings to our feelings, our love. That is the only proper soil that can yield true, fruitful, genuine human love, and this is the basis from which we discover what we have to seek as the innermost essential kernel in each individual.

"If we permeate ourselves thus with spiritual knowledge, our social life will be regulated in such a way that each single person, when he approaches any other in esteem, respect and understanding of the riddle of 'man,' will learn how to find and to regulate his relation to the individual.

"He who strives for genuine knowledge will find it, and will find the way to other people. He will find the solution of the riddle of the other person in his own attitude, in his own conduct. Thus we solve the individual riddle according as we relate ourselves to others. We find the essential being of another only with a view of life that comes from the spirit. Spiritual science must be a life-practice, a spiritual life-factor, entirely practical, entirely living, and not vague theory."[4]

6. Fundamental Ideas for Parents and Teachers

Harmonizing the Temperaments

By now it has become clear that each of the four temperaments represents a certain one-sidedness, even more so when it gains the upper hand and begins to dominate us, becoming less and less controllable. This gives rise to the question of whether and how we can help children, for example, so that they learn early on to control their main temperament. Are there ways to bring into balance, to harmonize, the fourfoldness that exists in each of us and that is often overpowered by one or two of the temperaments?

Rudolf Steiner addressed this question on the first afternoon of his abovementioned teacher training course,[5] after calling to mind the basics of his view of the human being. This relates to the fourfoldness that we discussed in the previous chapter: the four parts of our being. "Naturally, in the ideal human being, harmony among the four members of his human nature would reign, as foreseen by the cosmic order. ... One of the four elements predominates in every person, and it must be the goal of education and teaching to achieve this harmony among the four members."

In order to give every reader the opportunity to find out for him- or herself how the temperaments of two people affect each other, and in order to simultaneously discover the basic principle of all "schooling of the temperaments," let's take a concrete, easily understandable situation as a starting point.

How Should Children Be Seated in Class?

Rudolf Steiner emphasized how important it is to seat children in class according to their temperaments. But which temperaments are appropriate to seat together so they will have a positive influence on each other? We might think spontaneously of contrasting temperaments, for example seating a choleric child next to a phlegmatic one. Will the choleric child be able to harmonize her excessive temperament through him? Will she be able to gradually overcome it, to "wear it down," so to speak?

Let's imagine four different possibilities. For this, we'll choose the following class situation: Toward the end of the main lesson, the students have a text to copy from the blackboard into their main lesson books, and now they're told to put away their writing materials because the teacher wants to tell a final story.

1. A choleric child next to a phlegmatic one

How does the choleric react? "Oh boy, it's time for the story!" Open that satchel! In with the main lesson book! Stick the pencil case in! And the colored pencils! Done! Oh no! I forgot one! But it's not going in the case! Throw it in on top! So now I can hear the story!" The phlegmatic child next to her keeps on writing and writing – slowly – calmly – after all, he's not done yet – he hardly registered that the teacher said to put things away – he just keeps on steadily writing...

The choleric child sees him! How does she react in this moment? Is she delighted by his calmness, and does his behavior have a calming effect on her? Does the peaceable, leisurely manner rub off on her? She whose sole aim is to hear the story notices that her neighbor is holding up the whole business with his slow reaction!

That's impossible! She lends a helping hand! Snatches away her neighbor's book from right under his nose! Grabs his satchel! Sticks the book inside! Now in with the pencils! So the story can begin!

And what goes on inside the phlegmatic child? Does such conduct help him to harmonize his temperament, to be enthusiastic about being pressured so boldly, about active interference in his peaceful behavior? Will he want to imitate it and by so doing "wear down" his own temperament? Absolutely not. In fact, this could even serve to intensify his temperament, since he's forced to muster even greater calmness to cope with the disagreeable manner of his neighbor.

And that's something every adult who struggles with inner restlessness is familiar with: When you meet someone who's even more restless than you, it can give rise to a cheering feeling of superiority: "Thank God I'm not that bad," and this triggers a certain feeling of calm.

So, as a result of these observations, we can say that a choleric child seated next to a phlegmatic will not inwardly work on her temperament, and considering this, it is not appropriate to seat them next to each other in class.

2. A choleric child next to a melancholic one

What does the same situation look like if a choleric child is seated next to a melancholic one? We already know how things start out, but let's consider what happens when, while spontaneously moving her things, she accidentally bumps her sensitive neighbor who always moves so cautiously! When the melancholic protests, he hears only: "Don't make such a fuss! You're always so touchy! You're such a whiner!" – He starts to cry; he is frightened and uncertain; he beats an inward retreat.

This behavior is also unfamiliar and incomprehensible to the choleric child, though she may at other times secretly admire the thoroughness and beautiful bookwork of her neighbor. But there's no possible way she can imitate this!

And how does the melancholic child feel in this situation? "Now she really scared me. Does she always have to bump me like that? Can't she be more careful? Why does she always hurt my feelings? Maybe I should tell mama that I'm always afraid of her." For this child, too, his neighbor's behavior is not worth imitating: After all, he doesn't even understand when she complains about him or uses insulting language.

3. A choleric child next to a sanguine one

Let's recall how the choleric child resolutely packs up her things and then checks to make sure that her neighbor is working fast enough, too! But wait a minute, he's not in his seat? Oh, he's wandering around again! Where is he? Ah, back there! He's making arrangements for this afternoon. Typical! Now he's looking my way! "Hey, hurry up – get over here and pack up! – What, you've already got everything in your backpack? Sure, you copied everything again much too fast! Quick, sit down, the story…!"

This kind of behavior doesn't inspire her to curb her own temperament, either. Her neighbor doesn't take anything very seriously. And that's something she can't accept – something that can even get her angry! How can he be so superficial?!

And how does the sanguine student feel? He thinks: "I'm always so nice to her. I like to give her things, I like her and admire all the things she can do. But she's always so unfriendly to me, she scolds me, even hits me sometimes…"

So here, too, the temperaments don't have a harmonizing effect on each other.

4. A choleric child next to another choleric one

What's left now is to take a look at how two choleric students behave when they sit next to each other in class. Both want to be the first one done! One feels: "He always wants to be the first to finish! The show-off! When I'm faster, it really gets him mad! Sometimes he's really bad! It's unbearable! Then he even tries to pick a fight, even though I didn't do a thing to him! When that happens I could get so furious that I'd love to…" Well, the other one experiences everything the same way; we can put the same words into his mouth.

In the first three examples we experienced that, while the choleric student can get upset about the character traits of her neighbor, she feels at the same time affirmed in her behavior and superior to the others. But when she sits next to someone with the same temperament, something special happens, and this holds true for all four temperaments. It happens that she sees herself reflected in the temperament of the other; she is confronted with herself, unconsciously recognizes herself and dislikes her own characteristics that she sees in the other. In this process, the unconscious desire arises to become a different person, to "wear down" one's dominant temperament. This is similarly the case with adults, but they have to make enormous efforts to achieve what happens with children in an unconscious way when "like" is seated next to "like."

Now we can understand Rudolf Steiner's suggestion to seat children with the same temperament next to each other in class. Choleric children next to other cholerics, sanguine pupils next to other sanguine pupils, melancholic children next to other melancholics, and phlegmatic children next to other phlegmatics. (When talking about the phlegmatic child, he coined the phrase "to phlegmaticize." After school, however, phlegmatic children should play with different kids who have ideas and drive and will get them going.)

It sometimes happens that teachers are concerned that they might make a mistake with such a seating arrangement if they don't correctly identify a child's temperament. I always counter with the argument that one can only make a mistake by not doing this! Since everyone contains all four temperaments, an encounter always takes place with all four temperaments of one's neighbor. If we succeed in identifying one dominant temperament, or a temperament mixture, and we discover another child with similar characteristics, a corresponding seating arrangement creates a situation for both students in which they have the possibility to work on and harmonize themselves through the reflection that takes place.

Our study of a classroom seating arrangement has brought us much closer to the question of the basic principle for dealing with the temperaments. The crucial concepts that we will often hear, and which can serve as a key to understanding all that follows, can be summarized again. Hippocrates formulated the two laws: "Like *cures* like, like *identifies itself with* like." For the classroom we can conclude: "Seat like *next to* like."

The unconscious "reflection" that takes place leads to a deeply felt recognition of oneself. And it is this that induces our ego to begin an unconscious process within us, which leads to a gradual "wearing down" of the reflected temperament. As a result, greater and greater harmony can be achieved among the four temperaments over the course of time.

That Hippocrates' law, "Like cures like," is the basic healing principle of homeopathic medicine probably goes without saying. But our addition, "Seat like next to like," should not imply that we are talking about healing when we deal with the temperaments. It should be emphasized again that, as long as they do not degenerate and get out of hand, the temperaments have nothing to do with illness.

How can we understand this harmonizing even better? To illustrate, I can cite an experience I had with a friend of mine who was a forester. I had asked him to come over and give me professional advice because I had too many trees growing in my yard. At once he pointed out a big tree that towered above and cast shade on three smaller trees so they could not really thrive, and therefore stayed small and looked unsightly. He immediately started trimming the big tree so that the smaller ones had considerably more space and light. He predicted that in a few years I would be marveling at the greater harmony of the four trees. And he proved right.

Let's compare the big tree, towering over and suppressing the others, with the main temperament. It dominates the others and doesn't really let them have an influence. When it is "worn down," which is comparable to trimming the tree, the others can gain strength, have a better effect on each other and ultimately result in a greater harmonious unity together.

A further example can be cited that all of us can easily imagine: Within a group of employees, there is one person who always needs to make an impression, loves to be the center of attention and tries to dominate the others. And he doesn't even have to be the boss. The others are not really able to develop fully; they have to hold themselves back and thus feel repressed. When this individual suddenly goes on a trip or is absent for some other reason, the whole atmosphere in the group changes. Everyone breathes a sigh of relief, they reveal hitherto unknown aspects of their personalities and experience new harmony working together—until the trip is over. But let's assume that the person in question has a serious illness to cope with and doesn't come to work for a long time, and then returns as a completely changed person (such cases aren't as infrequent as you might think!): This situation can be compared to the "wearing down" of the temperaments. From now on, a new harmony can arise in the group, and the formerly dominant person can be integrated in a new way.

It is certainly justified to use the musical term of tones being "in harmony" when describing both harmonious human interactions and the harmonizing of the temperaments.

Putting a Seating Plan into Practice

Now that we've seen how appropriate it is to seat "like" next to "like," there are a few worthwhile practical aspects I have experienced that I would like to mention for the benefit of those intending to put such a seating plan into practice.

I usually reseated my students in all grades about four times a year. At home I formed an inner picture of every child, visualized the whole range of his or her shades of temperament anew each time, and then wrote them down so that four columns of differing sizes resulted. As a next step I considered the temperament mixtures and also the characteristics that were less prominent, and I made sure that the children did not always end up with the same neighbors. In this way it was possible to arrive at four groups of approximately the same size and then to place them appropriately in the classroom.

I let the sanguine children sit up front close to me, because they seek and need constant contact with the teacher, and I seated the choleric students behind them: They participate actively even if they are seated farther away. Whenever possible, I placed the melancholic children on the window side of the classroom because of the light—and the phlegmatic students too. The latter had their seats up front near me, so they sat in front of the melancholics.

If we imagine looking down at the class from above, there are always two temperaments sitting diagonally opposite one another. This was what Rudolf Steiner recommended, and it will become more understandable when we internalize the basics of his view of the human being.

Why the phlegmatic and sanguine children in particular should be seated near the teacher will be discussed in the next chapter.

93

But first let's stay in the classroom and answer that question by observing the child's relationship to the teacher, before going on to look at the home situation. The key to answering this was explained by Rudolf Steiner already in the early years of his work, especially in 1908 in his lectures about the temperaments which he gave in various places.[6] On the following pages I would like to refer to his words in more detail, since his remarks are very impressive and cannot be better expressed in my own words.

The Relationship between Teacher and Students

What do sanguine children expect of their educators?

In general, the sanguine child shows only temporary, fleeting interest in things, objects and events, but, as Rudolf Steiner states, "For a personality especially suited to a sanguine child— experience will show this—there will be a permanent, continuous interest, even though the child is ever so fickle. If only we are the right personality, or if we are able to bring him into association with the right personality, the interest will appear... Only by the indirect way of love for one personality is it possible for interest to appear in the sanguine child. If that interest, love for one person, is kindled in him, then through this love straight-way a miracle happens. This love can cure a child's one-sided temperament. *More than any other temperament, the sanguine child needs love for one personality.*"[7]

Here the teacher is confronted with the task of learning to conduct himself in such a way that his sanguine students not only like him and find him nice, but are able to *love* him! "Everything must be done to awaken love in such a child. Love is the magic word. Therefore parents and teachers must heed the fact that an enduring interest in things cannot be awakened by drumming it into the sanguine child, but they must see to it that this interest is won *by the roundabout way of attachment* to a personality. The child must develop this personal attachment. *One must make himself lovable to the child.* That is one's duty to the sanguine child. It is the responsibility of the teacher that such a child shall learn to love a personality." In other places Steiner used the following expression for this: "The teacher, the educator, has to learn to acquire lovable qualities."

We can conclude from this that these children are actually only able to learn well in school if they love their teachers, or at least really like them, and that constant unfriendliness, grouchiness, bad moods, stubbornness and arguing on the teacher's part spoil their experience of learning—one could also say of living. Now we can also understand even better why it is appropriate to have the sanguine children sit up front. They need to be close to the teacher; they want, for example, to quickly comment on or show us something, and they also expect us to be interested in everything they do.

But we are mistaken to assume that the educator should always be cheerful, happy, funny and in good spirits. From our own experience each of us knows which teachers we regarded highly. Weren't they the ones who, aside from being friendly, let us unconsciously sense inner human qualities such as love of truth, love of justice, level-headedness, etc., and by whom we also felt loved? So we have to work on developing ourselves to a certain degree if we want to be "loved" by others.

What does the choleric child demand of us?

Likeable characteristics? No, he can get along without those! He has no real feeling for things like that! Rudolf Steiner put it this way:

"Let us suppose that a parent should fear that in his child the choleric temperament would express itself in a one-sided way. The same treatment cannot be prescribed as for the sanguine child. The choleric will not be able to easily acquire love for a personality. He must be reached through something else in the influence of person upon person. But in the case of the choleric child also there is an indirect way by which the development may always be guided. What will guide the education here with certainty is: *respect and esteem for an authority.* For the choleric child one must be thoroughly worthy of esteem and respect in the highest sense of the word. Here it is not a question of making oneself loved through the personal qualities, as with the sanguine child, but the important thing is that the choleric child shall always have the belief that the teacher understands the matter at hand. The latter must show that he is well informed about the things that take place in the child's environment; he must not show a weak point. He must endeavor never to let the choleric child notice that he might be unable to give information or advice concerning what is to be done."

That, though, is no easy task. We have to learn to conduct ourselves in such a way that the child finds it possible to appreciate and respect us of his own initiative. It is so easy to develop disregard and disdain! If we let ourselves get a bit upset, for example, or even begin to express our feelings loudly, to shout or yell, the choleric child is quickly disappointed and loses all respect for us—after all, he can do that, too, and even unconsciously considers it a weakness. He wants to look up to us instead, to sense that his educator can control herself and cope with every difficulty without losing her composure. That is what the choleric child expects from us.

"The teacher must see to it that he holds the reins of authority firmly in his hands and never betray the fact that he is perhaps at his wits' end. The child must always keep the belief that the teacher *knows*. Otherwise he has lost the game. If love for the personality is the magic word for the sanguine child, then respect and esteem for the worth of a person are the magic words for the choleric."

What demands does the melancholic child make of us?

Rudolf Steiner: "Here it is of special importance that we do not build upon the possibility, let us say, of being able to talk him out of his grief and pain, or otherwise educate them out of him, because the child has the tendency to this excessive reserve. With the melancholic child it will be especially necessary for the teacher to attach great importance to showing him that there is suffering in the world. Here again there is a magic means. As with the sanguine child the magic word is love for a personality, with the choleric, esteem and respect for the worth of the teacher, so with the melancholic child the important thing is for the teachers to be personalities who in some way have been tried by life, who *act and speak from a life of trial*. The child must feel that the teacher has really experienced suffering. Bring to his attention in all the manifold occurrences of life the trials of your own destiny. Most fortunate is the melancholic child who can grow up beside a person who has much to give because of his own hard experiences. In such a case, soul works upon soul in the most fortunate way. If therefore at the side of the melancholic child there stands a person who, in contrast to the child's merely subjective, sorrowful tendencies, knows how to tell in a legitimate way of pain and suffering that the outer world has brought him, then such a child is aroused by this shared experience, this sympathy with justified pain. A person who can show in the tone and feeling of his narration that he has been tried by destiny is a blessing to such a melancholic child."

Here, too, it becomes clear that these children are not helped by amusing them and encouraging them to joke around, but by meeting them where they are and addressing their disposition: Through their ability to feel compassion we can divert them from *their own* melancholy and sorrow.

Here's a good example: In a fourth grade, a very bold choleric boy had become very angry about a melancholic classmate and therefore folded over the corner of a page in the boy's main lesson book. The latter began to cry about the ugly dog-ear, and when I came over to him, he was sitting there sobbing and inconsolable. I had him tell me the whole story and showed sincere interest, but now had the task of pulling him out of his deep sorrow. I had to tell him about even greater suffering and said: "Once I had a student who was so angry, he *tore a whole page* out of another child's book!" The sad fellow suddenly looked at me compassionately, realized how great the other boy's grief must have been, pulled himself out of his own grief, and commented that he really had been lucky in comparison. Then he got the idea of trying to iron out the fold. When I suggested that the other boy who caused the problem could do that for him, he was quick to explain that he would prefer to do it himself. We can recall that melancholic children have a great love of order; the other boy would not have done a good enough job to satisfy him. That's why he ultimately came up with an even better idea and said, "I'm sure that mama can iron it out best!"

What expectations does the phlegmatic child have?

After all that we've learned thus far, we will probably say: "Nothing," and that is no joke. Basically, he wants to be left in peace. But we can sense that we will certainly not do justice to a phlegmatic's development that way.

Rudolf Steiner said the following about it: "It is difficult to gain any influence over a phlegmatic person. But there is one way in which an indirect approach may be made. Here again it would be wrong, wrong indeed, if we insisted upon shaking up a person so inwardly at ease, if we thought we could pound in some kind of interests then and there. Again we must take account of what he has.

"There is something in each case that will hold the attention of the phlegmatic person, especially the phlegmatic child. If only through wise education we build up around him what he needs, we shall be able to accomplish much. It is necessary for the phlegmatic child to have much association with other children. If it is good for the others also to have playmates, it is especially so for the phlegmatic. He must have playmates with the most varied interests. There is nothing to appeal to in the phlegmatic child. He will not interest himself easily in objects and events. One must therefore bring this child into association with children of like age. He can be trained through the *sharing of the interests*—as many as possible—of other personalities. If he is indifferent to his environment, his interest can be kindled by the effect upon him of the interests of his playmates. Only by means of that peculiar suggestive effect, only through the interests of others, is it possible to arouse his interest. An awakening of the interest of the phlegmatic child will result through the incidental experiencing of the interests of others, the sharing of the interests

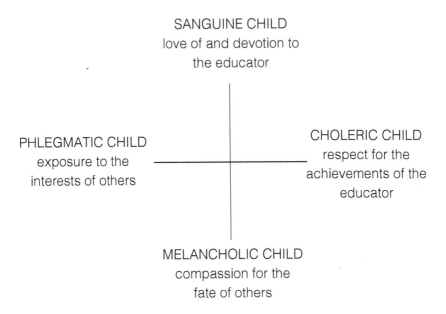

SANGUINE CHILD
love of and devotion to
the educator

PHLEGMATIC CHILD
exposure to the
interests of others

CHOLERIC CHILD
respect for the
achievements of the
educator

MELANCHOLIC CHILD
compassion for the
fate of others

of his playmates, just as sympathy, sharing of the experience of another human destiny, is effective for the melancholic.

"Once more: To be stimulated by the interest of others is the correct means of education for the phlegmatic. As the sanguine child must have attachment for one personality, so must the phlegmatic child have friendship, association with as many children as possible of his own age. That is the only way the slumbering force in him can be aroused. Things as such do not affect the phlegmatic. With a subject connected with the tasks of school and home you will not be able to interest the little phlegmatic, but indirectly, by way of the interests of other souls of similar age, you can bring it about. If things are reflected in this way in others, these interests are reflected in the soul of the phlegmatic child.

"Then also we should see to it that, particularly, we surround him with things and cause events to occur near him concerning which apathy is appropriate. One must direct the apathy to the right objects, those toward which one may rightly be phlegmatic. In this way quite wonderful things can sometimes be accomplished in the young child."

Now, if we reconsider the question about the phlegmatic's expectations, we can find an answer after all: The phlegmatic child unconsciously expects us to help him find friends who have diverse interests!

Rudolf Steiner summarized: "The sanguine child should be able to develop love and attachment for one personality. The choleric child should be able to develop esteem and respect for the accomplishments of the personality. The melancholic child should be able to develop a heartfelt sympathy with another's destiny. The phlegmatic child should be led to the sharing of interests of others."

On the basis of these explanations it becomes clear that the teacher must adapt to all four temperaments: indeed not an easy task, but a very interesting one through which she can learn, out of love for the children, to overcome any bias.

Suggestions for Working Appropriately with the Temperaments

From what has been described so far we can glean the basics for dealing with children and their different shades of temperament. Now we should ask what we need to know and observe in our concrete dealings with children who have one temperament that particularly predominates.

From Rudolf Steiner's words we can conclude that many subtleties and nuances matter. So Steiner's account will be cited here in numerous places.[8]

The Choleric Child

"If we have a choleric child to train, we must see to it before everything else that this child shall unfold, bring to development, his strong inner forces. It is necessary to acquaint him with what may present difficulties in the outer life. For the choleric child who threatens to degenerate into one-sidedness, it is especially necessary to introduce into his education what is difficult to overcome, so as to call attention to the difficulties of life by producing serious obstacles for the child. Especially such things must be put in his way that will present opposition to him. The teacher must put before him just those things upon which he must use his strength, things in connection with which the choleric temperament is justified. It will be especially good if these obstacles pertain to little things, to trifles, if the child is made to do something on which he must expend tremendous strength so that the choleric temperament is strongly expressed.

"Here it is necessary first of all to awaken reverence, the feeling of awe, to approach the child in such a way as to arouse such respect, by showing him that we can overcome difficulties that he himself cannot yet overcome. Reverence, esteem, particularly for what the teacher can accomplish, for his ability to overcome objective difficulties—that is the proper means. Respect for the ability of the teacher is the way by which the choleric child in particular may be reached in education."

From these words we can conclude that it would be wrong to make things too easy for the choleric child. We have to assign her tasks that require effort and strength, against which she can test herself and also use up her surplus energy. For example, in woodworking class she could be given a harder kind of wood (oak, for example) for carving so that she experiences resistance and has to overcome this obstacle. "In such a way, he gains respect for the force of things that stand in opposition to everything manifested by his choleric temperament," Rudolf Steiner adds.

Now let's look at how we could best react if a child has a fit of anger and even begins to lose control. For this case, Rudolf Steiner gave the following advice: "With the choleric child, try to become inwardly apathetic, to watch coolly when he has a temper tantrum. ... With no other method will you get choleric children to combat having fits of rage."

Here is a practical example: A boy in Grade 3 gets so angry with a classmate that he loses his temper, takes one of his colored pencils from him and breaks it in half. The two quarrel intensely with words, and the classmate cries. What should we do?

According to Steiner's advice, the teacher should under no circumstances become angry herself. One should calmly go over to the two and say to the angry child only: "You just broke his colored pencil." The other child will have to be consoled and told that he will get help to straighten things out. With the choleric child we should talk no more about it, but wait until the next day to do so, if possible before class begins, afterward if not—and in no way should we moralize! We should let him explain how the quarrel developed. "He got me mad, he stepped on my foot!" – "On purpose or by accident?" – "I think it was by accident, but it got me angry." – "Did he do anything else to you? Did he break anything of yours?" – "No, not that, but he got me angry, and then I really got mad, and then I saw his colored pencils lying there, so I took one and broke it." – "And how do you feel about it today, when you think about it?" – "That was not okay. I should not have done it." – "And have you thought about anything you can do to make up for it?" – "Yes, I'll buy him a new pencil – from my allowance." "Yes, that's good, but you also hurt him a little, and I'm sure he was very shocked when you did that." – "I'll tell him I'm sorry – and I'll draw him a picture, too." – "That's a good idea." At the end we should at least add a sentence in which we clearly express our own feeling that what happened was not right. And then end the conversation.

The fact that this kind of coming to terms with what happened is the only thing that helps in the case of infuriated children is something I once experienced in a drastic form while teaching, and I would like to describe this personal experience because it so impressively confirms what Rudolf Steiner said: I had a boy in my first grade class who got furious at the drop of a hat. When that happened, his face darkened and he began to go into a rant so that the rest of the class was afraid of him. In such situations I tried as calmly as possible, in the aforementioned way, to point out to him what he had done and what I had observed. He didn't calm down immediately, but usually began to grumble about and blame other classmates and was only gradually able to calm down. On the following day I had talks with him in the way I described, and ended them with the necessary concluding sentence. This went on for a number of years.

When this student was a twelfth grader, one of the girls from his class who was doing her senior project on the temperaments asked me to take her along to a public lecture I was giving on the topic outside of Hamburg. In the course of the evening I described an extreme example of the choleric temperament, and how I had tried to deal with the angry boy. In the car on the way home, the girl asked me if the boy I had portrayed was her classmate XX, which I carelessly admitted.

A few days later the boy approached me on the school grounds, greeted me cordially and said, "You gave a speech on the temperaments." – "Yes," I responded, and suddenly remembering with a start that I had revealed his name to the girl, I added with a guilty conscience: "But I didn't mention any names during my speech." He assured me that it was no problem and then asked: "Do you remember when I had my last tantrum in school?" I wasn't sure and let him continue: He hadn't had a tantrum since fourth grade; I had always had talks with him, and then at the end I had said something that he remembered. He could still very clearly remember my final sentence. I supposedly said to him: "You really don't need to do this any more!" I was of course very surprised and grateful for this acknowledgment. He also asked me if I had seated him next to classmate XY (he named him) because of his temperament, which I in turn admitted. (I had selected XY, who had strong choleric traits, to mirror him.) Our conversation ended with a comment from him that to me is an impressive confirmation of the seating method suggested by Rudolf Steiner: It was really very unpleasant for him to sit next to classmate XY because he couldn't stand the way he acted.

The Sanguine Child

To deal with a sanguine child, Rudolf Steiner gave two main suggestions. On the one hand, we should be sure to surround the child with many things that we have noticed to be of deep interest to him or her. "It will generally be easy to arouse interest in this or that subject, but it will quickly be lost again. There is one interest, however, that can be enduring even for the sanguine child. What is found to hold a special interest must be kept in mind." For example, if he has a pet that he is interested in, then by caring for it on a regular basis—collecting food for it, feeding it and giving it water, grooming it—he can simultaneously practice precisely the quality that he possesses the least of: perseverance. "Whatever he delights in, we must try to place in a special light. The child must learn to use his sanguineness."

On the other hand, we also expect to hear about the principle of having one's temperament mirrored or reflected in order to "wear down" the excess. This we discover in the following passage: "We should keep the sanguine child busy at regular intervals with such subjects as warrant a passing interest, concerning which he is permitted to be sanguine, subjects not worthy of sustained interest. These things must [for a short time – H.E.] be permitted to affect the sanguine nature, to work upon the child. Then they must be removed so that he will desire them again, and they may again be given to him."

We can think of all sorts of toys in this connection. It's fully appropriate for the sanguine to be interested in them for only a short time. What is of educative value and important for all parents of such children is the suggestion to skillfully take a toy away for a given amount of time and then bring it out again later, in order to arouse renewed interest (again, only for a brief time!). The child will then again be pleased with it, and we adults will have the opportunity to follow the child's playing more attentively—a good exercise in educating oneself.

"It is important to seek out for a sanguine child those objects toward which he is permitted to be sanguine. If we thus appeal to what exists (the sanguine) rather than to something that does not exist, we shall see—and practical experience will prove it—that as a matter of fact the sanguine force actually permits itself to be captured by serious subjects. That is attained as by an indirect path." This means at the same time that one doesn't attempt to ask her to be quiet and make her sit still for too long. As we learned earlier: Through her love and devotion to the teacher or to another person in her environment, the child will also learn to deepen her interests and, as a result, gradually achieve greater perseverance. "So we may say that it is best for the sanguine child if he may grow up guided by a firm hand, if someone can show him externally aspects of character through which he is able to develop personal love. Love for a personality is the best remedy for the sanguine child."

The Melancholic Child

Rudolf Steiner: "The melancholic child is capable of suffering, of moroseness. These qualities exist in him and we cannot flog them out, but we can divert them. Above all we must show the melancholic child how people can suffer."

About strongly melancholic children he says the following: "Such a child has the power within him to have a real propensity for hindrances, to cling to resistance/opposition." He creates problems for himself and doesn't want to or cannot tear himself away or actively free himself. "If we want to steer this peculiarity of his temperament in the right direction, then we must divert this power from the inside toward the outside."

So it means that we shouldn't try to cheer up or amuse such a child, but rather seize appropriate opportunities to show or describe to him how other persons—and animals too—experience sorrow. With his deep feelings he can put himself in other people's shoes and thus free himself, forget his own sorrow and learn to overcome his inclination to be reserved. The earlier example of the book with the dog-eared page applies exactly in this case.

"You should not divert him. In that way you will harden the gloominess, the inner pain. If you take him where he can find pleasure, he will only become more and more shut up within himself. It is always good if you don't try to cure the young melancholic by giving him gay companionship.

"Even in arranging the melancholic child's environment, so to speak, we should not leave his predispositions unconsidered. Hence, it is even advantageous if—strange as it may sound—we build up for the child actual hindrances, obstructions, so that he can be diverted by being directed to outer hindrances and obstructions. Then the child, the soul of the child, will gradually take a different direction."

When such children are older, one should tell them much about people who have had difficult fates and vividly describe how they accepted and coped with it. During adolescence it is good to give them biographies to read of significant figures who accomplished great things and experienced many obstacles and sorrow in doing so. We can help to divert their "inner feelings to the outside."

Some melancholic children always have the feeling that they are somehow special. In the classroom they realize that they can often answer questions that not many other students even attempt; they feel much more mature than the others; they do their written work much more carefully than their classmates; they have deeper interests and are much more thorough in everything they do. A certain degree of egoism can creep into the picture. For all of these traits, it is good if they hear a lot about other persons and their positive qualities. We should repeatedly give them opportunities to actively help others so that they can free themselves and stop focusing their attention on themselves.

The Phlegmatic Child

When dealing with the question, "What expectations does the phlegmatic child have of us?" it becomes clear from the comments of Rudolf Steiner that for the phlegmatic child it is of utmost importance to arouse his interests by the right kind of interactions with other children. This holds true especially at recess and in after-school activities. Now let's take a look at how teachers should behave toward such phlegmatic children.

Rudolf Steiner suggested to the teachers of the first Waldorf school that they should pay little outward attention to the phlegmatic children, but inwardly remain very clearly conscious of them. So we shouldn't look at them constantly but rather pay them little outward attention and not lose contact with them inwardly. How can we do this? "If you find access to his apathy, the phlegmatic child can be very interesting. But do not express this interest. Rather, attempt to appear apathetic. Try to split your being. If you have a lot of empathy inside, behave outwardly so that he gets to see a mirror-image of his own being [his phlegmatic nature – H.E.]. Then you will be able to influence his education."

We can compare this with a mother who has to leave her baby or young child at home while she goes grocery shopping, but constantly keeps him in mind, thinks of him and, despite everything, does not forget him. This is not easy, but we can practice it and learn to do it.

In this connection I made an interesting observation for which this suggestion was helpful and became more understandable: Often when I told my class stories, I noticed that the phlegmatic children sat there with a dreamy look on their faces and listened in their own way. If I approached them—they always sat in a group in front of me on my right or left—and looked them directly in the eye, it was like a small awakening for them, and they suddenly looked at me very attentively, forgot to listen to the story and were preoccupied instead with our looking at each other. This could even develop into a little looking game that can be described as: "You look at me – and I look at you…" So it was therefore best for me not to pay attention to them and to act outwardly phlegmatic toward them, barely interested.

Does this mean we should not concern ourselves at all with these children in class? "One can do the following, which is a surrogate but can help a lot: … Then one can achieve very much with them."

The point is not that the teacher forgets these children, but that she awakens and teaches them during short five-minute intervals by asking them questions or giving them tasks to solve— she activates them, so to speak. I was always astonished at all the things these children were capable of remembering, repeating or reporting on in this length of time.

A further suggestion: If parents are willing to try it and can make it possible, it would be good for such children to be awakened earlier and sent on their way to school earlier. Then they will already be much more awake when class begins.

"In the case of the phlegmatic it is important that one captures his attention from a different spiritual state." It is healthy for these children to change a habit quite often.

What we discussed more thoroughly in the previous chapter about pursuing new interests should be repeated here again for the sake of completeness: "The phlegmatic is reached best if we produce in him an inclination toward the interests of other personalities, if he can be stirred by the interests of others."

7. Suggestions for Storytelling in Class

Telling a Story Vividly

It quickly became obvious to the participants of the first teachers' training seminar that Rudolf Steiner intended not only to inspire and encourage understanding of the different temperaments, but also to give many practical suggestions in connection with this topic for teaching all lessons. Let's begin with what Steiner had these teachers practice from the very first day: how to tell a story.

At the end of each day's main lesson, the class teacher tells a story: In the first grade they are fairy tales, in the second fables and legends, in the third Biblical accounts from the Old Testament, in the following two grades sagas and myths of the Norse, then of the Greeks, and then finally vivid accounts from ethnology and Roman history. Aside from this, many other topics are related by depicting them in as vibrant a way as possible. Now let's consider which narrative style might be the most appropriate for each of the different temperaments.

A choleric teacher whose choleric temperament predominates will certainly tell a story in a completely different way from one with mainly phlegmatic characteristics: She loves to make a story exciting and describe things dramatically, perhaps moving back and forth at the front of the classroom, suddenly speaking more loudly, increasing the intensity of her words and possibly even letting the whole inner drama become visible in her facial features, like an actor. The more phlegmatic teacher, on the other hand, speaks much more slowly, pauses between sentences and describes things calmly and peacefully without any drama, like an epic poet.

These two contrasting styles make it sufficiently clear that one will not inwardly reach all the children with these two ways of telling a story, and that's why Rudolf Steiner suggested that teachers should learn to find a suitable narrative style for every temperament. This means that in the course of telling the children a story, one has to learn to portray one part cholerically for the choleric children, another part phlegmatically for the phlegmatic children, and so on for the other two temperaments. When a story is told this way, all the children naturally immerse themselves in each of these four different moods, which is quite all right, since everyone has all four temperaments. But in the passage directed at his dominant temperament, the "mirroring" or reflection we have spoken of takes place unconsciously in the child, which at the same time encourages the ego of the child to "wear down" this temperament.

The same holds true for the way we discuss and review the contents with the children after telling the story. On the next day or the day after that, we let the children retell the story, which is a topic we will look at later.

Let's first take a closer look at these four different styles of storytelling. First, a few comments from Rudolf Steiner on this topic: In his first teachers' training course in 1919, he assigned individual teachers the task of reading a story for the following day and telling it to the others in such a way that it was effective for a certain temperament. After hearing these stories he gave suggestions: "The teacher should develop the natural, intuitive ability to treat the child according to his temperament. ... But one does not discuss a story until one has had the children retell it."[9]

If we sum up Steiner's later comments on storytelling, the following aspects are most important:

For the melancholic children, one should create a warm, pleasant, cozy mood when telling a story. One describes details in the story in such a way that the melancholics are impressed by them, especially when the details have to do with aspects of the outer world. It is also good to show them something from time to time that they can evaluate and judge, and they will feel particularly involved if there is something fateful or tragic in the story in which they can take a deep interest. While telling the story one can express many aspects in the form of questions, which encourages them to reflect, and one shouldn't forget to frequently use elaborate sentence structures with intertwining elements. The language of the storyteller has to be powerful, but not too strong.

For the sanguine children it is important to depict many, many details, to enumerate wherever possible in the story. One should tell the story fluently and a bit more quickly than for the other temperaments. They can also be shown things again and again, so they have something to look at that will keep their senses active. It is also good to insert small breaks now and then, because this will force the children to let their attention drop and then reawaken it again afterward. Also, they will maintain their attention much better if we keep an eye on them while telling the story. The sentences can be formulated in such a way that many commas and semicolons are used. This creates the feeling of a freely flowing, carefree river with a couple of rapids.

For the phlegmatic children we should select a calm, steady-paced narrative tempo. We will describe only a few things, but thoroughly and in a drawn-out way, using repetition and complete objectivity. Once in a while a pause is effective, preferably before an important word or happening, so that the children briefly continue to think about and imagine what might happen next—but then the story continues differently. We should construct sentences that contain dashes, like little pauses for breath. An example for telling fairy tales in the first grade: "The princess – she was – very beautiful – but – not so – good!" The other appropriate punctuation mark is the period: Short sentences in which the melody quickly rises and then falls again. This technique is particularly effective because it arouses curiosity and the necessary interest. When telling a story, the teacher should be conscious of how important it is for phlegmatic children that the stories arouse new interests, as varied as possible.

For the choleric children one attempts to construct short, clipped sentences, the kind that often end with an exclamation point! The result is a dramatic narrative style with much suspense and many impressive events. Rudolf Steiner used a comparison: Telling a story should be like pounding posts into the ground; he used the expressions "to pound in stakes" or to tell a story "in pushes and shoves." The most important elements in this type of description are brief sentences, direct speech, imperatives, exclamations and the present as narrative tense. Verbs should dominate, and sentence openings emphasized frequently; the language used is firm, hard, even sharp, sometimes dangerously quiet and sometimes intimidatingly loud.

Steiner gave the following advice for dealing with a conspicuously choleric child: "With a raging child one should steer the attention to fabricated situations.... Choleric children go into an inner rage against things that they are expected to comprehend."[10]

Here Steiner draws attention to the fact that choleric children do not understand some things quickly, get inwardly agitated— today we would say aggressive—and vent in angry outbursts. So it is important for them to hear dramatic stories in which they can experience images of courageous deeds. Steiner gives another example on this topic that one could further embellish in the manner described: A horse has broken out of his stall, and a brave person (boy, girl, woman or man) wants to capture it and manages to, after a number of adventurous attempts and dangers.

With all four narrative techniques, it is also important to articulate very differently—loudly or softly, brightly or darkly, slowly or quickly—and create both suspense and resolution, an easing of tension.

How a Teacher Prepares to Tell a Story

How does one prepare for telling a story in this way? One could go to work on just one temperament and follow the abovementioned suggestions for a few weeks to practice a technique at certain spots in the story one is telling. Then one goes to work on a second temperament and practices only that one, and so on for the others. Finally, one tries it with two, then three, and when one has practiced long enough and attempts all four, one prepares the night before in the following way:

First we read the story—a fairy tale, fable, or whatever—and familiarize ourselves well with the content. Then we decide which portion is most suitable for the choleric children and which ones for the other temperaments, and we try to get into the correct mood. When starting out we could also briefly practice coloring the passages according to the respective temperaments, but after a while this is no longer necessary! Only the next day will we very trustingly tell the story in the four different styles in the order practiced—as well as we can.

It might not be easy at first to identify the different aspects and then decide on them. Here are a few ideas that might help:

For the melancholic children, select portions of a story about people which will appeal to their deeper world of feeling: where sorrow and distress are involved, where people help or sacrifice themselves for others, where someone experiences something fateful.

For the sanguine children, choose passages in which there is a lot to observe, where the outer world is described and rapid changes happen; where there is a lot of activity and speed; where a wide variety of things is listed.

Devote passages to the choleric children in which powerful, dramatic and exciting things take place, where something difficult or significant is achieved and where the deciding factor is drive and, above all, courage.

For the phlegmatic children, select parts in which something takes place calmly or slowly but can be depicted in an interesting way. Very often there is such an opportunity when an easing of tension is necessary after an exciting occurrence.

Once we have decided, a few notes can be jotted down and, if necessary, placed on our desk the next morning or held inconspicuously in our hand. Already after a short time this will no longer be needed, but such little aids are helpful now and then for the inner security and confidence of the storyteller.

A Practical Example:
The First Ascent of Mount Everest

In the seventh grade geography class I tried to acquaint my students with the Asian continent, and when looking at and drawing the map, they were very impressed by the mighty mountain ranges with the highest peak on earth. So what was more natural than to tell them about the first ascent of Mount Everest? I read the impressive accounts of the expedition and the two mountain climbers, Hillary[11] and Tenzing.[12] The evening before class, I thought about how I could divide up the various parts so that the next morning I could do justice to each temperament. What then took place every day in front of the children—the impromptu slipping into a fourfold way of describing—I will now try to express in writing.

The Ascent

1. The First Part

At the beginning it is important to describe a lot of details to introduce the children to what is happening. For this, the sanguine narrative technique with its quick succession of images and enumerations is the most appropriate, because it allows us to progress quickly. At the same time this style also has the effect of getting all the children listening, involved in events, and vividly imagining what is being depicted. After a few introductory words we can tell the excerpt in the following way, following the descriptions of Edmund Hillary:

For the sanguine children:

At the beginning of March in the year 1953, everyone meets in Katmandu: The men of the expedition to Mount Everest, experienced mountain climbers, Sherpas, the many porters, half of whom are women. The two main characters are there: Edmund Hillary from New Zealand and Tenzing Norgay, a Sherpa and native of the region—they are experienced mountaineers who have already tried and failed once, but they don't let themselves be discouraged. They have never met before, but these are the two who alone will succeed in attacking the summit.

On the 10th of March they begin their trek to the foot of Mount Everest. Everywhere people line the paths and wave to them. They hike for 17 days in perfect weather through the beautiful countryside of Nepal. They go swimming in the rivers, eat hearty meals and sleep under the starry night sky.

Quite soon they set up a base camp: Camp One. Altogether they will set up nine camps along the way. They stay here for a while. They want to practice everything together, learn how to work with all the equipment, how to use the new "oxygen breathers," how to set up and take down the different tents and efficiently pack the baggage, distribute it among the individual porters, and on and on and on ... From here they go off into the nearby mountains in groups of three or four, for days on end. They learn to climb, chop steps into the ice with their ice axes and explore glacier valleys, practice crossing glaciers with crevasses, even climb a few 20,000-foot peaks and get used to breathing the air, which gets thinner and thinner.

Hillary and five of his men get a special task from the leader of the expedition, John Hunt, whom Hillary greatly admires: They should explore the dangerous Khumbu glacier that is extremely difficult to negotiate, find a safe path through the breaking ice and look for locations for Camp Two and Camp Three.

For two days they make plans, get tents, rope and hooks and snap hooks together, figure out how much food and fuel they will need, check the Sherpas' equipment and hire porters for the Khumbu glacier. On April 9th the six men leave the Thyang Botschi monastery—the last safe spot—accompanied by five experienced Sherpas and 39 Sherpa porters, half of them women, who were hired in Nepal.

Then it snows. They realize that they haven't taken along any snow goggles for the Sherpas. If they keep going, the porters could get snow-blind! Oh, what luck! A few of the men have wide skiing goggles along with replacement lenses made of celluloid, and Stobart is talented and constructs a pair of "sample goggles." He has the men make 30 copies of them and saves many men's vision. They happily call these goggles "Stobart's specials."

Then they can move on in high spirits. They twist their way between narrow towers of ice, leap over cold glacial streams and bypass swaying ice formations along the way. Already on the same day, after great exertions, they set up a base camp at the foot of this region of breaking ice. Hurray, we did it! The second camp is set up. Here they pay off the porters, who happily turn homeward. But the men of the expedition only reluctantly take leave of these brave fellows and women. They have a lot to thank them for. What would they have done without these valuable helpers?

In a few days the expedition moves on. The path becomes more and more exhausting but they don't give up. They give special names to certain spots of the glacier that put particular obstacles in their way—names like "Mike's terror," "Hillary's horror," "Atom bomb field," "Hell-fire alley."

How could it be otherwise? They are able to find the right location for the next camp, and some of them say it is really ideal. How happy they are that everything has gone so well so far! Then the other groups arrive, and there's a merry reunion.

Many more days will pass until they reach "Camp Nine," their last and most lonely station, but the day will come, they all hope, when Hillary and Tenzing will start out from there to reach the summit!

2. The Second Part

After the great push forward, it's time for a break. That happened automatically from time to time because of the heavy snowfall, which had a calming effect but also covered over the tracks and firmly packed paths which were necessary for those who would follow.

Hillary often describes what a great feeling it was for all of them when they crawled into their tents at night and could finally slip into the protective cover of their sleeping bags. Snowstorms sometimes even forced them to take breaks lasting a number of days. An ideal passage for the phlegmatic children!

For the phlegmatic children:

It's starting to snow again – and it snows and snows and snows – without stopping. That means: No moving on – looking for a camp ... There it is – good – now bend down – slip into the tent... Wait, first check out the ropes – very carefully, of course – a snowstorm could come. Good, now they are all tight – yes, they will hold, even in a storm – now brush all the snow off my clothes – down with the head – crawl into the tent on all fours. Aha, most of the others are already here – I'm quite often the last one – but not this time. This time I was faster than some of them – here they come ... Now everyone's here, thank goodness! Not a single one is missing! And now we don't have to go outside anymore ... The other day we had to do a search and go back outside, for a long time... Now I can pick the pieces of ice out of my beard – that's no fun – the hairs stick to the ice. How great, the cooker is giving off pleasant warmth! The water will be boiling in a minute, much faster than at home – it already smells like tea – someone passes me a mug. Oh, that tastes great – ah, nice hot tea! That really warms you up and the warmth goes right through you ... How good that feels! And now: Peace, nothing but peace. That feels really good – and is also necessary – after all this strain...

The men have done their day's work. They hadn't planned to go any farther today. "Thank goodness the snowstorm didn't begin earlier," says Hillary. "Make yourselves comfortable. You deserve it." The rest of the snow on their clothes melts and melts – so do their stiffly frozen beards. The men become more talkative – and they loosen up, chat – make jokes, laugh, make themselves comfortable – as far as possible. In the meantime the food is prepared. The smell of it causes excitement... Yes, they're very hungry and thirsty – and the food tastes very good!

Outside the storm is raging – gets stronger – but they sit here in the warm tent – and feel safe! Let it storm as much as it likes: It will calm down at some point. Fatigue overcomes them. Soon they will crawl into their sleeping bags. Wait – the plan for the next day has to be discussed first. They have a lot ahead of them – in case the weather permits. The more religious men thank the Lord – pray – think of home... and... fall into a deep sleep. Outside the snowstorm is raging, shakes the tents, but our mountain climbers feel secure. Let it snow more tomorrow – then they'll have another day of rest. What a pleasant feeling!

3. The Third Part

The ninth and last camp has been set up. The decisive day has arrived! Only two men dare to do it and manage to do it: Edmund Hillary and Tenzing Norgay. What stresses and strains and obstacles lie ahead of them: Danger lurks everywhere! It won't be possible without oxygen masks. A few other mountaineers made it up this high, tried to go on a bit farther, but then had to turn around again. Today is the big day: It's now a matter of conquering the mountain of all mountains! This is a passage for the choleric children!

For the choleric children:

It's 6:30 in the morning! Two men crawl out of their tents. The summit already glitters in the sunlight! Only nine more miles to the summit – but over a thousand-foot difference in altitude. That's going to be difficult! They put on their backpacks and oxygen breathers – the tubes have to be attached! At last there's enough air – how marvelous! "That gives me hope!" Hillary says. Put on the crampons, the irons used for climbing, and take the ice axe! Between them is the indispensable rope. The ascent can begin!

Steep slopes ahead – with deep powdery snow! You can't stop Tenzing, he makes his way ahead! He leads both up onto the snowy shoulder of the glacier. Steep and dreadful the southern summit looms over their heads! Tenzing pulls ahead – cutting his path through the snow – then Hillary takes the lead. Changing positions again and again!

The crampons grip firmly into the hard wind crust. Suddenly Hillary breaks through the ice – up to his knees! First of all, stop for breath! Carefully pull out one leg first, then the other… "That was really lucky! A broken snow crust is the mountain climber's worst curse!"

For a whole half hour: Nothing but tramping on ahead – really strenuous! Then: "The snow conditions are getting better!" There's a hollow! And two snow-covered oxygen containers! "So Evans and Bourdillon got this far. On the way back we'll have enough oxygen!" What unexpected luck!

"The ridge is getting steeper! We have to get up there!" Tenzing should take the lead – and does so. But he, too, breaks through the ice crust – at first just up to his knees! Then again: this time up to his hips!

Now it's Hillary time to lead. "What a dangerous slope!" A piece of ice crust six feet wide gives way, and Hillary slips down with it – three or four steps! "Stay where you are," Tenzing cries out. Too late! Hillary says to himself: "This is Mount Everest, mate! You just have to get through this!"

Fatigue! They have to stop to rest – and to confer. Tenzing's got to decide if they can go on. His answer, as always: "It's okay with me!" What an important phrase! They won't give up, won't turn back, they are going to make it!

Suddenly the going gets easier. Firm snow! They can thrust their ice axes into it, and they hold!

At 9 o'clock they stand on the southern summit. Rest – drink – relax! "Don't waste any time!" Then they go on! First they head a bit downwards again. To do that, they have to chop steps in the ice – how tiring! Now up a steep wall! Hillary paves the way – attached to the rope. Tenzing follows!

Now they're close to the summit! Now carefully carve steps into the snow! "The snow is firm." – "Just a few more strokes of the axe, just a few more weary steps, and we were standing on the summit of Mount Everest!" wrote Hillary in his diary.

4. The Fourth Part

While the two men are attempting to conquer the last leg without the company of the others, their friends remain back in the various camps, hoping and worrying, and imagining how hard it must be to manage the ascent that grows steeper with every step while carrying such heavy equipment. They hope that everything will go well, and ask themselves anxious questions—again and again. They can imagine the strain and feel deeply for the two men. This is a situation that would be especially suitable for a melancholic description.

For the melancholic children:

Particular tension reigns in the second-to-last camp where the mountain climbers firmly shook everyone's hands when they left yesterday. On the following day those waiting are able to follow the ascent of the two men for a while with their binoculars, and see how they leave Camp Nine early and how they take turns leading and then following one another. Hopefully, they will always have snow or firm ice under their feet and won't step into a crevice or a snow cornice – a huge piece of snow that protrudes out over the cliffs and breaks off when stepped upon – and then crashes down into the depths! Where can they be now? Will there be enough oxygen for breathing? Will they even have enough strength? Will the two men, who have pushed themselves so hard the last few weeks, be able to stick it out and ultimately reach the summit? They'll also have to be thinking about the descent, which everyone knows is even more difficult because they will be in constant danger of slipping and falling into a ravine. One of them could barely pull the other one out without losing too much precious time. What would happen if Tenzing Norgay were not there – the fellow who gathered such important experience when he accompanied an expedition to Mount Everest two years ago and can now put it to use?

"We can only pray that nothing unexpected happens to them and that the mountain allows these two humble men to be the first to step on its summit. We shouldn't even think about all the dangers that lurk along their way, and by tonight we will know if everything went well because they have to climb over nine miles up and then down on the same day; otherwise they will freeze to death."

"Which of the two will reach the summit first, Hillary or Tenzing?" asked the men who had a hard time controlling their inner tension. Some thought that Hillary would definitely be allowed to go first, because he was the leader of the expedition. Others thought that Tenzing might be quicker and have more strength in the end to be the first one on top. "I am sure that both of them will take the final decisive step together at the same time. That would suit them best," said one of the men in Camp Nine. "Wouldn't that be noble of them? Each needed the other, and one man alone could never have done it."

How astonished they were when they heard that it wasn't at all important to the two who stepped first on the summit! Tenzing modestly stayed back and let Hillary go ahead. Hillary was the only one to take a photo. Up there he took a series of pictures of the landscape, but only one single photo of a man, and on it Tenzing could be seen hoisting a flag. Both were deeply grateful that they had succeeded together – and later they became the closest of friends.

On the Summit

Here we can again let three different temperaments have a say and then use the fourth temperament when describing the subsequent descent. From the way the description is formulated, the reader will certainly recognize which temperament is being addressed.

What an accomplishment! They did it! And they can hardly believe it themselves. Two men who didn't even know each other before! They are overwhelmed by their feelings and can hardly express them! Hillary shakes Tenzing's hand in great recognition! That's not enough for the Sherpa – Tenzing throws up his arms and embraces Hillary tightly! They give each other a slap on the shoulders – a vigorous slap! They had reason enough to be satisfied! Yes, and they were very proud, too! They deserve to be proud: They were the first men to reach the earth's highest summit!

How did the two of them feel up there? From the impressive account that Tenzing wrote later, we know that he was a deeply religious man, a Tibetan Buddhist, who had spent his whole life waiting for this moment. He speaks of "his mountain" and emphasizes that for him it wasn't a lifeless mass of rock and ice, but a warm and well-meaning living being. To him, the mountain seems like a hen and the other peaks like chicks under her wings. As a devout Buddhist and a Sherpa conscious of traditions, he is full of gratitude and inner emotion at this unique moment and wants to express his deep respect to the gods of this mountain. They also need to hoist the flags they have brought along, which certainly wasn't easy to do in the ice, snow and very thin air. But he also remembers how his little daughter Nima had bid him a sad farewell – not knowing if her beloved father would return – and given him a pencil to bury for her on the summit. He scratches a hole in the icy crust of the summit and entrusts his offerings to the mountain: some zwieback, chocolate, a little crucifix from John Hunt and, on top, some pieces of sugar for the gods who inhabit this summit. They will be covered by snow, sink deeper and deeper and from now on belong to the mountain that they are thanking for this success. Soon they will have to start thinking about the descent, which is known to be much more difficult than the ascent. How will that go?

But that's unimportant right now – they stand – they have arrived at the top and look out – look out calmly into the distance – in all directions … They try to internalize the images they see – and take the oxygen bottles off their backs at least for a few minutes… Oh, how good that feels! Hillary takes picture after picture … It's difficult with the thick gloves – Tenzing waits patiently … Now he should hold the flag up high over his head – for the photograph. It's hard to breathe … very hard … without oxygen. But they want to save as much of it as possible … so, take deep, slow breaths … Tenzing had a camera, too, but in the excitement he'd left it back in camp. He could have taken a photo of Hillary … but they won't have that now … Maybe he's never taken a photo before, thinks Hillary – but he doesn't have time now to show him how – the weather is incredibly beautiful … "Feathery clouds moved across the sky, and the valleys below were covered with cotton wool," wrote Hillary later in his diary. But now they first need to rest ... at least for a few moments ... They scratch out a hollow in the snow to sit in, nibble with pleasure on the sticks of rock candy – a pleasant tiredness overcomes them ... Now they could sleep and sleep, sleep deeply – stop, that's not allowed! So, get up ... put the oxygen tanks back on, open the valve ... "Oh, that feels great!" Fresh air fills their lungs ... wakes them up ... now it's time to take leave – "We have enough oxygen for only two hours."

The Descent

Oh, it's not even twelve noon yet, Hillary happily discovers as he anxiously checks his watch. They begin their descent at exactly 11:45, quickly recognize the way they came, see the steps that they carved in the ice during their ascent, and try to use them again as they head down. How easy this is, they think, and hope that it will go on like this! They feel light-hearted. If they have had so much luck so far, why shouldn't the mountain let them get back down from its summit just as easily without anything out of the ordinary happening? Even if they sometimes slip or slide or face a dangerous situation: There is nothing that can distress them. Of course they cannot be careless or even too high-spirited. They immediately recognize the dangers that lurk everywhere, call each other's attention to them, call out to each other or communicate with sign language. Oh, what a joy that they are making headway much faster than they had thought!

Nevertheless: Haste seems necessary, and so they speed up their step, soon reach the edge of the cliff, let themselves down the chimney on ropes, but immediately act cautiously wherever the descent is too steep. They carefully creep over a narrow belt of rock to the steps in the last steep slopes, and then something surprising occurs: During a short break, Hillary offers a drink from his own canteen to his loyal companion whom he has come to hold in high esteem, who saved his life in the crevasse during the ascent, and who has been at his side without the least complaint. And how our Sherpa enjoyed it! And later he told about this incident over and over again, because in retrospect it was this moment that seemed to signal the beginning of a long friendship. The otherwise taciturn Hillary offers him a swig from his canteen, and time and again people asked Tenzing about the special drink and imagined that it must have been something very special if a friendship of such distinction resulted from it. And it was with great delight that Tenzing responded to all these curious questions: "It was a mixture of water, citric acid and raspberry juice!"

The two of them again take up their ice axes, take turns leading; on their way down they tramp down steps that they both carved out of the ice on their ascent that morning, and Hillary experiences how difficult it is for him to use the very wide steps that Tenzing had made. He often has to use his ice axe to help him reshape the steps, and in doing so expends a lot of precious energy so that he sometimes feels that his strength is fading. But look – Tenzing descends behind him in good spirits, beams at his new climbing friend with a broad smile, and that has its effect on Hillary, who is therefore able to stick it out quite well to the very end.

They bravely leap over precipices and have to perform a variety of feats that seem daring, and then feel really grateful when they find the two oxygen bottles and can hook them up. They both beam with joy and don't even want to think about what they would have done without them. From this point on they have to withstand a number of violent gusts of wind and even put up with being bombarded by icy hail, but none of this can even shake them in the least.

There – they can hardly believe their eyes – they're already near the camp, they see a tall figure approaching them and quickly realize that it's George Lowe. The joy of seeing him and then all the others again is almost indescribable. The whole world will be talking about it; all the newspapers will report this, and so one can hardly wait to hear the reports of the two men who succeeded in climbing to the top of the world's highest mountain with its 29,000-foot peak. Hillary closes his diary with the comment that for him, Tenzing's joyful, victorious laughter on the summit of Everest will remain unforgettable – the Sherpa with whom he will share a true friendship.

A Brief Review

In this narrative, each temperament is addressed twice, albeit in passages of different lengths. Here and there in daily teaching practice one would of course spontaneously "color" one or another passage differently—especially if one notices that the narrative style we just discussed is not easy to handle or needs to be changed sooner. After a bit of practice one develops the necessary feel for these things.

Another teacher would probably divide up this story completely differently, and that is completely justified! What is being expressed here should not be understood too schematically.

On a given day, we may also not be able to employ all the different characteristics of narrative style. In the above version for the melancholics, much in the first part, for example, was "expressed in the form of questions, by which the children are encouraged to reflect," and "fateful aspects" were addressed. In the second part, on the other hand, very few questions were used and more emphasis was placed on "more elaborate sentence structures with intertwining elements."

When narrating for the sanguine children, it very much matters that we stand facing them, keeping an eye on them and showing them something once in a while to have an effect on their attentiveness. We attempted to use what was described above in the following words as the characteristic narrative style: For the sanguine children one selects passages in which there is a lot to see, in which the outside world is described, rapid transitions take place, there is a lot of quick action, and many different things are enumerated. The sentences can be structured with a lot of commas and semicolons, especially with the long lists of descriptions, so that the story moves forward quickly and lightly.

With the descriptions for the two other temperaments, the narrative flow can be made much more obvious in writing by way of distinctive punctuation: The exclamation point reveals the choleric style, the hyphen or the ellipsis the phlegmatic style.

With this example I have attempted to describe an impressive experience by using as many passages from the author (Hillary) as possible, and to transform these in the process so that the temperaments became obvious. But when telling about a historical occurrence, we could also rearrange and further embellish individual sections for the children quite freely, building up a story that addresses all the temperaments. A very successful example of this can be found in Peter Lipps' account[13] of "The Crossing of Columbus," which I often refer to in my seminars. I also frequently have the participants spontaneously tell the story in four different parts that are colored differently for the four temperaments.

Letting the Children Retell the Story

As was indicated at the beginning of this chapter, one lets the children retell parts of the story the next day or the day after. Now one has to decide: Which children should retell which part? During the lesson, the principle of "like heals like" was observed. Now it is interesting to note that Rudolf Steiner suggested that a different principle be followed the next day. One doesn't let the choleric children retell the dramatic conquest of the summit, but gives them the phlegmatic depiction of how the men enjoy the coziness and comfort in camp.

It should be the phlegmatic children to retell how Hillary and Tenzing reach the summit by summoning up all their strength, feeling and relating to the drama of the situation and being creative in their formulation of the story. The same holds true for the melancholics and sanguines. The melancholic temperament can retell the sanguine beginning of the story with all the details, so that the child turns her awareness outward and occupies herself solely with events in the outside world, while it is good for the sanguine child to put himself in the shoes of the men in Camp Eight with all their inner questions and worried thoughts and then retell this in his own words.

So they slip into the temperament that is least visible in themselves. In doing so, they have to become active and creative, which is something altogether different from listening to the teacher's story. The harmonization takes place through their own conscious activity, while when listening everything takes place unconsciously.

In what follows we will see that Rudolf Steiner takes up the aspect employed here in other connections as well.

8. Further Suggestions for Teaching the Main Lesson

We can deal with the temperaments not only at the end of main lesson when we tell a story, but also whenever we describe or portray anything. The diverse subjects taught in main lesson offer a wide range of possibilities to be creative in "coloring" the subject matter according to the temperaments. Let's focus here on a few examples from animal and plant study, geography and chemistry as well as English, and at the same time develop the method and the theoretical basis for adapting our storytelling and work on other topics with regard to the four temperaments.

Teaching that is oriented to the temperaments is, of course, only one of the many pedagogical aspects that we need to consider.

Animal Study

Animal study begins in the fourth grade, and the class teacher learns about the special way it should be dealt with in Waldorf teaching during his or her training or from related literature.[14] Here we will focus on how one chooses a selection of animals that will be dealt with and described for the children in a narrative way that is "colored" according to the temperaments. For example, we can ask ourselves: What animals can we describe in such a way so that the sanguine children, then the phlegmatic children, and then the other two temperaments feel especially involved?

For the Sanguine Children

Here the focus is on finding an animal that is particularly fast, can move, climb and jump quickly (maybe even from tree to tree), skillfully evade danger, swiftly and smartly seek food and consume it accordingly, etc. These would all be characteristics that the sanguine children can easily identify with, because they behave in the same manner. Such animals exist in all regions of the world. The squirrel will probably come to mind at once, but there are also other rodents that display similar behavior. Among the predators there are also similar creatures that sanguine children can easily relate to, for example the weasel or marten.

When preparing such a description, one should research all the essential aspects of this animal in a biology book to get a comprehensive picture and be able to translate this with all its details into a sanguine narrative the following day. In the subsequent class discussion, in which the contents of the lesson are discussed in more detail with the children by asking questions, one does not have to stay in the sanguine mood. But it is important that we give the *melancholic* children the opportunity the next day to recall as many details as possible. In doing so, they will have to turn their inner perspective outward and interest themselves in the world around them.

For the Phlegmatic Children

Which animal is particularly appropriate for the phlegmatic children? It would have to be one that moves quite slowly, is somewhat ponderous, makes a calm and peaceful impression, perhaps also likes to eat a lot, spends a lot of time doing this and digests slowly. Most probably one will immediately think of a cow lying on a pasture and ruminating. But with some modifications one could also choose an elephant, rhinoceros, whale or other peaceful animal and then describe them with their characteristic traits. The following day we should let the *choleric* children recall the details.

For the Choleric Children

If we want to bring the choleric children animals they can relate to, the important aspects are easy to find. We need only imagine animals characterized by activity, aggressiveness, rapaciousness, dramatic pursuits and hunting habits, quick capture and greedy devouring of prey—and we will easily find the corresponding group in the animal kingdom: the predators—lions, tigers, etc.—but a bull or bison could also be described dramatically. The recall on the following day is done by the *phlegmatic* children.

For the Melancholic Children

What animals can we find for these children? They love to remain hidden; they love silence, peace, quiet and solitude; they seek protection and security; they are shy, cautious and reserved. We also find these behavioral patterns in the animal kingdom. When we describe such animals to them, they can empathize deeply and see themselves reflected. We could for example think of animals that like to live in lairs or subterranean dens or up in trees, or that always seek the security of the forest: marmots, deer, badgers, foxes, moles. During the subsequent recall, it is the *sanguine* children who should slip into this element and describe the animal against the background of this mood.

A Few Comments on Methods

Since describing an animal in class takes a considerable amount of time and one cannot describe several on a given day, one might ask if this doesn't mean that we have to deviate from the basic principle of addressing all the temperaments every day. This is not at all the case. So how can we simultaneously address all four temperaments when describing a squirrel, for example?

If we describe the way this animal moves, there is no possible way we cannot feel sanguine, and this feeling should indeed be relished in detail. But then we can turn to the melancholic children by lovingly describing how it builds its nest and cares for its young, and then mentioning how secure the young animals feel. A dramatic passage for the choleric children would be to depict how the squirrel also has enemies and how it has to fiercely defend itself against an attacking marten, but how it is nevertheless able to escape through its great skillfulness. We tell the phlegmatic children how these animals hibernate in winter and occasionally leave to seek out the hiding places where they buried nuts the previous fall, how they find some of them and then leave the rest as seeds that nature will let grow.

This same method can be used to describe all animals. One can always find some point of view for coloring the individual passages in certain ways. For this to really work, what is important here is to choose the appropriate passages the night before while preparing the next day's lesson, and make note of things for the next morning.

The following diagram summarizes what we have just discussed and at the same time can be helpful in the search for contrasting animal species when we are choosing descriptions. We can describe the agile rodents in a sanguine way. When we describe the predators, the choleric children will listen particularly intently; the melancholic children will be able to empathize with animals that need the protection of a lair or den, and the phlegmatic children will enjoy focusing their attention on peaceful ruminants on a pasture (we could also include herds in Africa).

To prevent any misunderstanding, I would like to make clear at this point that the temperaments are, of course, a typically human concern. They are elements that are reflected in nature. We can use them as a bridge in order to be able to slip into the different ways of telling a story.

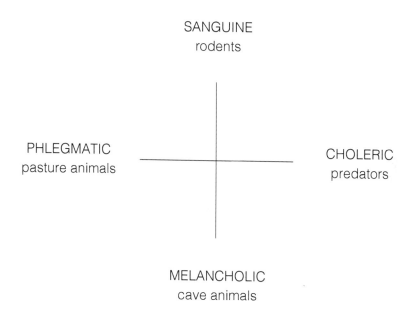

Narrative Styles and the Elements

If we want to describe something for choleric children, we have to get ourselves into the mood that corresponds with the element of fire, which means that we have to become warm, fiery or even hot inside—depending on the intensity of the topic we are relating. From time to time, sparks should fly when we talk! For the sanguine description we have to slip into the air element and become inwardly light, lively, vivacious and quick. We reach children with a phlegmatic temperament when we enter into a flowing, streaming, regular inner movement that is like water. The earth element has a close connection to form, and we will particularly reach the melancholic children when we form and structure our sentences well, using elaborate and complex expressions.

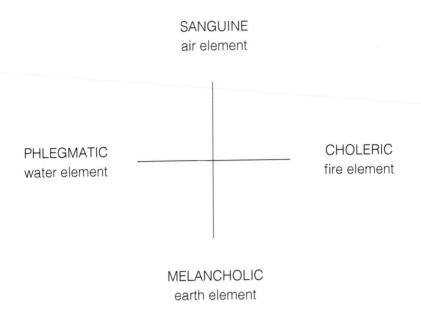

SANGUINE
air element

PHLEGMATIC
water element

CHOLERIC
fire element

MELANCHOLIC
earth element

Fish

Let's take a further look at the animal kingdom and consider how we could describe fish, for example. Since different species have different names in each country, let's concentrate on a few general aspects so that we can select appropriate species on our own.

There are fish that dart quickly and briskly through the water, that like places in rivers where the water surges over stones and bubbles and sprays, those that even leap out of the water, and others that constantly stay together in huge schools and spontaneously change direction together—the kinds of fish that sanguine children love.

Others swim very slowly, eat in a leisurely manner, feed on plants and are very peaceful. There are even some that like to settle down on the ground—the kind of description the phlegmatic children can identify with.

Fish that like to hide alone among aquatic plants, avoid being seen or even bury themselves in the mud, and others that like to lead a solitary existence and are therefore true loners can really win the hearts of the melancholic children if they are described in the appropriate way.

And, finally, the choleric children are impressed by the predatory fish with their constant pursuit of prey, the danger they represent, their unpredictability and voracity.

Birds

We can also discover variations in the bird kingdom that make it possible for us to use different narrative styles. It would probably suffice to imagine the four most important kinds of birds: songbirds, birds of prey, water birds and waders.

It will be easy to describe the songbirds in a way that makes the sanguine children feel particularly involved with their singing, cheerful chirping, early waking and ensuing morning concerts, their blaze of colors and rapid and graceful flight. What an impressive experience it is to watch a lark take wing vertically and hear it sing!

How different is the bird of prey, for example the eagle! It soars highest of all and circles majestically! Suddenly its sharp eyes discover a little yellow chick—even at a distance of miles! Like a bolt of lightning it begins its steep dive, closes its wings, goes faster and faster, and brakes just above its prey! And its sharp claws are already gripping and seizing its prey, its hooked beak pecking and biting! At once it soars up again—the king of the skies! Just right for the choleric children.

We watch a duck swim at a leisurely pace, in no hurry at all, dipping its head in the water once in a while and swallowing a

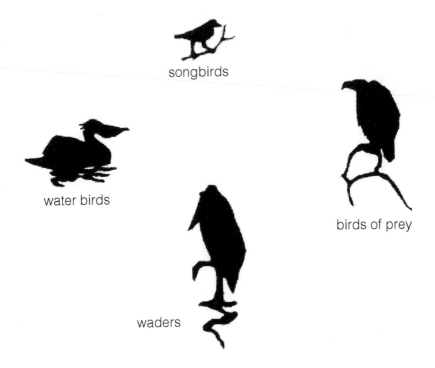

songbirds

water birds

waders

birds of prey

bit of food, soon afterward resting peacefully on the water, grooming its feathers, and finally sticking its head under its wing. In the case of water birds, it's the phlegmatic children who feel most involved.

When we see a wading bird striding along we are immediately reminded of the gait of a scholarly professor lost in thought. Let's imagine a stork or a crane: With raised head it struts along upright, deliberately, yes even with solemn dignity, and often remains standing in one place in a swamp for a long time, gazing into the distance. When it searches for food, it bends its long neck, lowers its relatively small head into the water, and skillfully finds what it perceived from above without the least sign of greediness. For the melancholic children we can use the narrative style especially appropriate for them to vividly describe such birds.

142

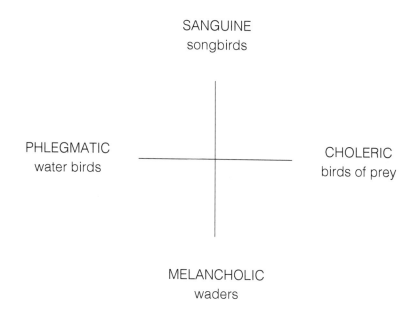

SANGUINE
songbirds

PHLEGMATIC
water birds

CHOLERIC
birds of prey

MELANCHOLIC
waders

The silhouettes on the preceding page give a visual impression of what we just described. They were drawn by C.A. Feldmann (The Hague), who called them "The Four Temperaments in Bird Form." The example of these four groups of birds makes it especially clear that they have a connection with the four elements, which are also the basis for the four narrative styles.

Botany

Two examples will demonstrate how we could create descriptions for each temperament when studying botany. First, let's look at four types of trees and then take a look at the structure of plants.

Trees

We'll try to give four characteristic descriptions of trees so that every reader can find further appropriate types that fit into each category.

To arouse the enthusiasm of sanguine children, trees should have airy, light, mobile qualities; thin branches that easily move to and fro in the wind; small, well-formed leaves that rustle in the slightest breeze and turn beautiful colors in fall. The wood will be succulent and fresh and have a nice grain. We may think at once of the white *birch* tree. But these characteristics apply to the aspen and other trees as well.

For the choleric children we could describe trees that have a knotty, gnarled quality and whose branches grow at sharp angles, as if they want to go in a different direction every year. Some trees even have a special connection with the fire element: Their bark is used to tan hides to make leather—using a procedure equivalent to a mild fire process. This is the *oak* with its fingerlike leaves and extremely hard wood. As already mentioned, experienced woodworking teachers give this kind of wood for carving bowls to choleric children who need to expend excess energy.

We could describe trees for the melancholic children whose branches hang down low as if they were sad. Many of them grow beside creeks, bowing down as if they were lowering their heads, and letting the tips of their branches touch the surface of the water. Over the course of years their trunks grow hollow, and the old wood decays inside and turns into soil. In these trees the earth element predominates. It is particularly the *willows* that we are talking about here, but other trees also exhibit such mournful forms.

Now we still have to find a tree species for the phlegmatic children. For them we could describe trees that develop thick trunks and mighty treetops over long periods of time, with so many branches and boughs and leaves that they form a remarkably dense canopy. It seems that they possess much more life force than the other species, and many specimens grow very old. The *linden* tree is such a tree. In Germany in former times, they were planted in villages and small towns on the village square or marketplace, and—when they were big enough—a circular bench was often placed around their trunks where people enjoyed sitting in the evening to chat with their acquaintances. Many kinds of birds nest in their treetops, and when the tree comes into blossom, we can hear a buzzing and humming from morning to night: Countless insects, above all bees, find especially tasty nectar here. Yes, the linden tree has such a superabundance of sap that, in the summertime, it constantly lets some of it drip down on objects below. So we can see that these trees have a connection with the water element.

Plant Growth and the Four Elements

When we describe how a plant such as a rose develops from root to blossom and then bears fruit, we can do so in four stages that show an interesting connection with the elements:

1. Root formation as connection with the earth – an anchoring in the earth element;

2. the rhythmic growth of stem and leaves – a process in which the water element plays an important part;

3. the opening of the colored flower corolla and the stamen; here the air element is particularly active;

4. the formation of the fruit and seeds, in which the fire element has special importance.

We begin by telling about the seed that germinates in the earth, forms a small upward shoot and at the same time begins to connect itself with the soil through its tiny roots, which make their way downward and remain there in the darkness unpretentiously; they want to serve to give our rose a firmer and firmer footing. We can "color" all these aspects appropriately in our description for the melancholic children.

In the second stage what matters is that our rose shoot breaks through the surface of the soil, forms two seed-leaves and then begins to develop its central stem and the stalks and leaves that grow in regular intervals along it. For this growth with its upward- and downward-flowing sap, our rose—like every plant—needs much water. Let's observe its growth: It grows a bit upward, then takes a short break and forms a leaf bud, then grows upward a bit, stops again and forms a further leaf. This goes on until it stops growing completely and brings forth a flower bud on the end of the stem. If we now take a look at such a fully developed rose shoot from above, we will discover that the rose has formed its leaves in a certain rhythm, in stages: Each new leaf appears at a point two-fifths of the way around the central stem. Once the fifth stage is reached, it produces a leaf in five different places that looks like a five-pointed star, a pentagram, from above. When describing this, one inwardly addresses the phlegmatic children with their water element and tries to arouse their interest for this geometrical relationship. When we describe growth and leaf formation, it is easy to slip into the phlegmatic narrative style, because it is about a constant repetition. We can also describe the process by saying that the plant contracts when it forms the stem and then expands with every leaf it produces.

Now we have arrived at the rosebud. At first there are five sepals wrapped around the blossom, which must ripen inside their protective covering. Then these open and five wonderfully colored rose petals develop fully like the wings of a butterfly, stretch up and turn toward the light of the sun, wonderfully fragrant. Golden stamens begin to open and hold out their golden pollen for insects. Many visitors are expected, and there is plenty to eat. All day long there is humming and buzzing! The pistil with its ovary and stigma stands proudly in the middle of this wonderful form. Like every plant, our rose wants to expand and disperse its scent when blossoming, offering itself completely to the world around it. Air and light are the elements of the blossom, and it won't be hard to find the narrative style to arouse the enthusiasm of the sanguine temperament for this stage of the plant.

After the blossoming comes the formation of the fruit! The ovary swells, grows, and develops into a brightly colored fruit. In the case of the rose, it even has a name of its own: the rose hip. The warmth of the sun lets it ripen and grow. Inside the shiny fruit the opposite takes place, but this remains unseen by the human eye: Here the plant gathers and contracts all its life forces, concentrates them in a mysterious way and thus forms seeds for the future. Fruits can be soft and juicy and taste delicious to humans and animals, but the seeds inside are dry and not tasty for us. It seems as if the sun with all its warmth has lured out all the water and "baked" the seeds, so to speak.

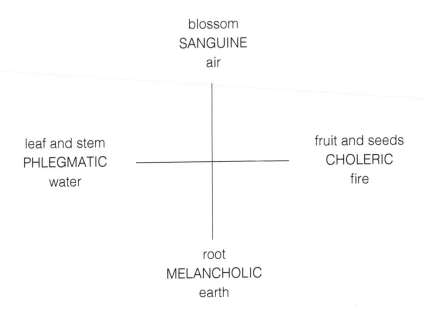

At this stage fire plays the decisive role, and it makes sense to tell the choleric children, in the appropriate narrative style, about fruit and seeds, describing exactly how they look, how they feel to the touch, how they taste, how they are harvested, which animals feed on them, etc.

In this or a similar way we can arouse the children's interest for all kinds of plants, and by using the different narrative styles we can allow them to identify more strongly with what we describe.

Geography

Geography is another subject that lends itself particularly to teaching children through graphic descriptions and storytelling. We can describe our earth's diverse landscapes and how their inhabitants live and work. We talk about different native peoples, and also about the lives of explorers and discoverers. In doing so, we have countless opportunities to use the four elements to address the different temperaments.

When we studied the pictures that my students drew of the Hallig islands, some readers may have thought that living in such solitude cannot be very easy for sanguine children (though sanguine children are born and raised there, too!). But it is not this kind of observing that we do in geography. Instead, we use our fantasy to slip into the different landscapes and, like an artist, "color" or paint them for a particular temperament when we describe them.

An art landscape, with its constant change of ebb and flow, with its calm, serene inhabitants, their fishermen and their boats, can be well represented in a phlegmatic style. Also suitable are descriptions of rivers, lakes, oceans and those of large forests with their greenery as well as the wide green steppes of other countries, where the water element is silent.

We address the choleric children by describing landscapes in which fire plays a major role: volcanoes and their powerful force. But there are also other dramatic aspects of nature that can be depicted in a choleric manner: dangerous cataracts in major rivers; precipices and chasms in mountain ranges; towering rock formations and peaks; crashing surf and storm tides on the coasts; deserts fraught with danger.

We can have an impact on melancholic children with descriptions in which expanse and vastness or remoteness and isolation become tangible for them: in regions of perpetual ice, in deserts, high mountain ranges, on islands, on the oceans. We should also describe episodes from the lives of explorers who accomplished significant things through their bravery and exceptional efforts.

For sanguine children we describe landscapes by talking about the people who live there and reporting on their work, habits, homes and cultures. They feel particularly involved when they hear about delightful, hilly, varied landscapes, and they are especially interested in the different peoples of the earth. They love to study maps and be given the assignment of imagining a trip and then taking it together with their class—as each student follows the route in his or her atlas. On such a trip, the children are allowed to travel by train, ship or airplane.

Geography offers an infinitely abundant field of study with all its portrayals of landscapes, not to mention scenes from the lives of indigenous peoples and the explorers and discoverers. An imaginative teacher will have no problem addressing the four temperaments again and again based on the four elements.

Phlegmatic: the green of the steppes, the green of the forests, the great rivers, the expanse of the seas...

Melancholic: perpetual ice, towering mountains, loneliness, endlessness...

Choleric: volcanoes, cataracts, breaking surf, high peaks and deep chasms...

Sanguine: low mountain ranges, settlements, the changing courses of rivers, human activities.

Chemistry in Grade 7

As a further example of how the class teacher can make students aware of the elements while taking the temperaments into consideration, let us take a look at one of the first chemistry lessons in Grade 7, which focuses on the topic of "fire."

After having observed a big wood fire on the first two days of the main lesson and showing the students how differently the various parts of a tree (twigs, leaves, roots, thick and thin branches) burn, we also let them observe how a fire looks at the edges of its flames, in the middle and at its base; we then point out that there are four kinds of fire.[15] These have a relationship with the four elements, and we can therefore say that fire exists in "earthly," "watery," "airy" and "fiery" forms.

We then burn four different materials in front of the children, beginning with small charcoal briquettes or pieces of coke. We place these in a suitable container on the experiment table and hold the lighted Bunsen burner above the black pieces. It takes a long time for them to ignite, and when small flames finally appear and we remove the Bunsen burner because we think a fire is now burning, we see the fire retreat inside just to glow. The children describe this as a quiet, unassuming, inconspicuous fire that is withdrawn into itself and hardly noticeable from the outside. The melancholic children hear expressions that they subconsciously associate with themselves. We can call this an "earthly" fire.

In a second experiment we take denatured alcohol and attach a wide board to a ring stand so that it hangs slanting downward with its end over a sink. Then we darken the classroom and pour a tablespoonful of denatured alcohol onto the board, and it begins to flow downward in a wavy pattern. We hold a burning match above it, it ignites, and the flames flow leisurely downward in the same wavy pattern. We let the students describe what they see and then repeat the experiment after turning off the lights, in total darkness. How impressive: We see slowly flowing, blue flames wander in a wavy pattern toward the sink, and after all the flames have disappeared, we discover traces of water on the board, left by the alcohol. The children feel that we should call this a "watery" fire—the element of the phlegmatic.

In a third experiment we hold a medium-weight paper shopping bag above a gas burner that is turned on but not aflame and fill it with the escaping gas, while pressing the opening of the bag firmly around the burner. Once it is filled we quickly remove it with both hands, take it over to a nearby burning candle, and then squeeze the gas-filled bag all at once so that the gas rushes toward the flame. It immediately ignites, and a flaming ball of gas can be seen for a moment. The children describe the characteristics of this kind of fire: fast, fleeting, like lightning, light, bright; we call it an "airy" fire. This is the mood corresponding to the happy-go-lucky sanguine.

A fourth experiment will show the students that there are earthly materials that possess such a strong fiery force that they cannot even be extinguished with water. For this we take an empty old tin can and fill it halfway with petroleum. After taking the necessary precautionary measures (a bucket of sand for extinguishing, protective goggles, maintaining an adequate distance), we ignite the petroleum, and powerful flames rise from it. How can we extinguish this fire? With water, as we are accustomed to? We attempt it: From a distance of six feet we squirt water into the flames with a spray bottle, but the flames don't go out and get even bigger, and because the sprayed water immediately evaporates and spreads into the surrounding area, one has to keep a safe distance. Even with a lot more water, a petroleum fire cannot be extinguished, but a shovelful of sand immediately puts it out. Such an experiment and its result really impresses the cholerics. "That's awesome, thrilling, exciting!" they say. We can call the petroleum fire a "fiery" fire.

In the chemistry lessons we do two of these experiments on one day and then let the students describe them. We should not discover the four elements in these experiments until the following day, and by no means right after the experiments.

English Class

Poetry

In the course of a school year, we have students learn a whole series of poems by heart in class. In the selection of these poems, too, we can take the temperaments into consideration.

We reach the sanguine children when we select poems that are to be recited rapidly and focus on something that is happy or merry. There are words that express a certain lightness, like the verb "flit" or the adjective "freckled." Even individual consonants have different characters, and the way we pronounce an "F" corresponds to the sanguine temperament.

The following poem, which we recite in the early grades—of course with all the children—and accompany with suitable gestures, can serve as an example:

> Freckled fishes, flirting, flitting,
> Flashing fast or floating free,
> Flicking filmy fins like feathers,
> Feeding from the flowing sea.

Choleric children like it when actions are described that demand energy and resolve. Verses and poems about people who work manually, about diligent craftsmen like the strong blacksmith depicted in the lines below are particularly appropriate. The triple "clink," the repetition, the use of exclamation points, active verbs and forceful intonation are characteristic of the choleric temperament. The sounds that particularly reach cholerics are "G" and "K."

The blacksmith, the blacksmith,
So big and so strong...
He hammers once,
He hammers twice...

Clink, clink, clink shall my anvil ring
And this is the way my hammer will swing...

Go, go, gallant good knight, gallop over the ground,
Give the gift of thy great heart's gold
Till the Grail's gold thou hast found.
Cold, cold, the cruel king, cold the crystal cave...

We touch a particular chord with phlegmatic children when we recite poems with them that depict calm events or slow animals and characters. For the early grades, we select a finger play that deals with a very sleepy dwarf whose imperviousness to wakeup calls arouses the indignation of even the strongly phlegmatic children. The calm description with its use of repetition, the "S" sound and its extremely slow presentation are good for these children.

In a mountain very deep,
A little dwarf is fast asleep.
The sun goes up so very high
And shines so brightly in the sky.
"Wake up, wake up, you sleepy head!"
(The dwarf is sleeping in his bed.)

Then comes the birdie Peep-Peep-Peep:
"Wake up, wake up, you sleepy head!"
(The dwarf is sleeping in his bed.)

Then comes the beetle Creep-Creep-Creep
And creeps into the mountain deep.
He pinches dwarfie on the nose.
"Achoo! Good morning,
Good morning, good morning!"

Melancholic children love it when a poem or rhyme expresses something serious or intellectually stimulating for them to think about, even if they perhaps don't yet understand all the finer nuances. They pay particular attention when the topic has to do with outer and inner light, and they like to recite poems slowly and thoughtfully, in keeping with the contents. They also have a special inner relationship to vowel sounds. When we read the following lines from William Blake, in which deep wisdom is expressed in a few words, we can sense that to a melancholic child they can be a great help for a whole lifetime.

Joy and woe are woven fine
A clothing for the soul divine.
Under every grief and pine
Runs a joy with silken twine.
It is right, it should be so
Man was made for joy and woe,
And when this we rightly know
Thro' the world we safely go.

A poem can also address more than one temperament. In the following we experience the optimist who affirms life (the sanguine) and the pessimist who at first negates everything and then is able to have a positive experience after all (the melancholic).

This poem can also easily be acted out in class. There will definitely be many children who would like to be one of the frogs while the rest of the class recites the whole poem.

The Two Frogs

Two froggies sat beside a stream;
both of them had had a dream.
The first one said: "The world is great,
so many mosquitos on my plate!"
He jumps for joy, spreads out his toes,
merrily hopping off he goes.
The second one said: "The world is bleak,
there's nothing good for me to seek."
He drops his head, sinks in the sludge
and from his dark hideout doesn't budge.
But then the lovely sunshine is there
and thousands of mosquitoes fill the air.
The gay frog snaps, then gulps them down,
delicious mosquitoes from all over town.
Through muddy sludge the rays of sun
warm the dark hideout of the other one.
And that is what the other frog needs;
he takes heart and looks up through the weeds.
He paddles up and croaks away,
which means the same as "Good day, good day!"

Poetic meters

A further possibility for dealing with the temperaments presents itself if we look not only at the content of the poems to be recited, but also see them in connection with four different meters. By reciting rhythmically with the children, we can help them to harmonize their temperaments in this way. This suggestion can also apply to recitation in foreign language classes.

The rhythms that begin with an unstressed syllable, a "short," we call "rising" rhythms, and those beginning with a "long" or stressed syllable, we call "falling" rhythms. The rising rhythms are appropriate for choleric and sanguine children, the falling ones for melancholic and phlegmatic children. In class we should pay attention to alternating between verse forms that rise and fall, and we can of course also recite other poetic meters that are not directly associated with the temperaments.

For choleric children we select the *iambus*, a meter with a short and a long syllable:

short - long; short - long; short - long; short - long

U — U — U — U —

The earth is firm beneath my feet,
The sun shines bright above,
And here I stand – so straight and strong,
All things to know and love.

For the sanguine child the *anapest* is especially appropriate—beginning with its two unstressed syllables and then leading into peace and calmness with the long stressed syllable that follows. In the first few grades we clapped this rhythm very often, sometimes with no words, and an amazing thing happened: It really calmed the children down, and they were able to listen and pay attention much better afterward:

> short - short - long; short - short - long
> U U — U U —

> Brave and true will I be
> Each good deed sets me free –
> Each kind word makes me strong
> I will fight for the right,
> I will conquer the wrong.

> *Spring Poem* U U —

> Pan doth play
> Care away
> Fairies small
> Two foot tall
> With caps red
> On their head
> Dance around
> On the ground
> He's no bard
> Who cannot sing
> The praises of
> The flowery Spring.

We take the *trochee*, consisting of a stressed syllable followed by an unstressed one, for the melancholic children. With the initial long syllable we meet the children in their state of inner stillness and then with the short unstressed syllable lead them out of themselves a bit, with not too strong an outward movement:

> long - short; long - short; long - short; long - short
> — U — U — U — U

Sword of Michael brightly gleaming
Down to earth its light is streaming –
May we see its shining rays
In the Winter's darkest days.
                              – Norah M. Ward

Tyger, tyger, burning bright
In the forests of the night ...
                              – William Blake

Advent

Now the twilight of the year
Comes, and Christmas draweth near.
Man and beast and bird and flower
Waiting for the midnight hour
Waiting for the Christ-child's birth
Christ who made the heaven and earth.
                              – Ann Ellerton

The phlegmatic child we will meet with a long, stressed syllable. The *dactylic* meter contains three syllables, the first one accented followed by the second and third unaccented. This is particularly suited to this temperament. We first address the phlegmatic with the long stressed syllable, and s/he then needs the two short syllables to really get moving:

long - short - short; long - short - short; long - short - short
— U U — U U — U U

Evangeline

This is the forest primeval,
The murmuring pines and the hemlocks ...
                              – Henry Wadsworth Longfellow

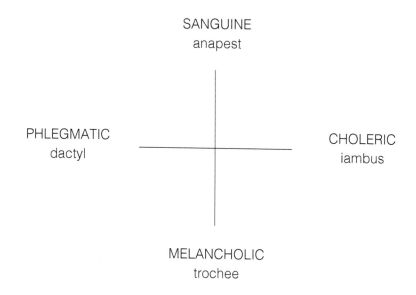

By the way we present these four verse meters to the children according to the four temperaments, it can again be seen that we always try to meet them where they are inwardly and then lead them into the opposite realm with its contrasting characteristics. We can address the sanguine and choleric children's joy of movement with the short syllables and then lead them to rest, while we do the opposite with the melancholic and phlegmatic children.

Storytelling in the Eighth Grade

Following the Waldorf curriculum, the class teacher in Grade 8 will work with his or her students on identifying four main writing and narrative styles of famous authors on the basis of the temperaments. The students investigate the diverse narrative styles of great authors in order to determine which temperament might be characteristic of each style (not the content). The teacher thus faces the double task of introducing the students to the basics of the temperaments, as well as working with them to find out what features are typical of the different narrative styles. So we first attempt to convey to the students a lively impression of the most important qualities of this quartet, and of their combinations with neighboring temperaments.

Since the four elements were already discussed in chemistry class in Grades 7 and 8—how they played an important role for the Greeks in recognizing universal laws—the students are now asked to place the temperaments in relation to the elements. They quickly discover the choleric connection to the fire element, and in the sanguine temperament they see the happy-go-lucky, flighty qualities of the air. Finally, they also realize that gravity—or the earth element—weighs heavily on the melancholic, while the phlegmatic individual has inner fluid processes, for example the lymphatic system, to thank for his or her composure.

In a second step, we try to find stylistic features in writing based on this knowledge.[16] The assignment requires the students to study and experience the various styles while learning to feel how a writer constructs sentences and which temperament might be expressed in sentence construction. Thus the class pays attention to the form—not the content or meaning—of a narrative text. To begin with, I demonstrate how one can tell a story in four different ways, colored according to the temperaments, as the class teacher has already done for years in order to address the different groups of children. After that we turn to examples from well-known literature.

The first thing the children took note of in my presentation of the texts was the choleric narrative style, which they summarized in their main lesson books: brief sentences – much direct speech– frequent exclamations, therefore many exclamation marks! – use of present tense – verbs dominate – the beginning of the sentence is emphasized – the language can sound firm, hard and harsh.

All this immediately becomes obvious when listening to the first stanza of Schiller's ballad "The Hostage" (*Die Bürgschaft*):

> The tyrant Dionys to seek,
> Stern Moerus with his poniard crept;
> The watchful guard upon him swept;
> The grim king marked his changeless cheek:
> What wouldst thou with thy poniard? Speak!"
> "The city from the tyrant free!"
> "The death-cross shall thy guerdon be."

With a few words, Schiller communicated a whole story in one single stanza – it's hard to imagine doing it any more succinctly!

Based on my description of the sanguine temperament, my students were able to identify many characteristics – sometimes with a bit of help. Their notes reveal that descriptions are light and breezy – the sentences literally bubble out – curiosity is aroused – there is a lot of description: what one hears, sees, tastes – one feels a lot of movement and mobility – the impressions change rapidly – the narration seems effortless – details are given about what one can see, hear, smell, taste and feel. In a similar way, characteristic features of phlegmatic and melancholic styles can be discovered.

It can be very interesting to let the students write a story of their own in the different narrative styles. One time we chose the following subject: A person has overslept, but has to catch a specific train (or another means of transportation) on time. What funny stories resulted! The children didn't always succeed in focusing only on sentence construction. But they did slip into the other temperaments, so that a choleric student – who often nearly exploded with anger when he arrived late – had to describe how a phlegmatic person did not get at all upset when he overslept, but very calmly waited for the next train – without rushing at all. Time and again, these exercises were the source of a lot of laughter and amusement.

Dealing intensely with the temperaments while studying narrative styles during an eighth grade English main lesson block is a time of deepening self-knowledge for both teacher and students. The students become aware of their dominant temperament or combination and recognize typical characteristics in their classmates and their teacher. But I always avoid talking with students about their own temperament, since that would make these young people feel insecure and unsure of themselves. This main lesson block definitely has a particular importance within the eighth grade year.

In summing up our diverse suggestions on how to deal practically with the temperaments, we can say that teachers are offered a wide range of possibilities in the various subjects to deal with these four character types and, in the process, to help children overcome their imbalance or one-sidedness. Teachers who work in this way will also experience that they become more creative and skillful as a result, learning to organize and design lessons in a more lively and artistic way.

9. Viewpoints on Parenting

The Temperaments in Family Life

Everything that has been said thus far about the teacher's personal way of dealing with students' temperaments also holds true for family life. In what follows, let's take a look at the temperaments in different family situations.

The Sanguine Child

How pleasant it is for a sanguine child if the adults at home respond to her with kindness, friendliness and cheerful faces! After all, she is usually charming and likeable, and because of her love for father and mother, such a child can learn to do the chores and tasks that have been set for her. And this in turn means that with time, the child will gain more staying power, develop greater perseverance, and in this way overcome excessively sanguine characteristics.

A mother or father who is also quite sanguine will find it easy to behave kindly and cheerfully, enabling a mutual mirroring of these characteristics so they have a harmonizing effect on each other. However, such parents must work on themselves to be able to demonstrate perseverance. A family environment that is not overly phlegmatic can also provide the sanguine child with ample pleasantness and good will.

It will not be so easy, on the other hand, for melancholic and choleric parents to respond to the sanguine's love of life with enough cheerfulness and understanding, since—in keeping with their own temperaments—they will be quick to find fault: A melancholic parent will tend to criticize the child for not doing her work thoroughly enough, and a choleric parent will get angry at her for starting a lot of things but not completing them.

With phlegmatic parents, the sanguine child will feel good. She will be given a lot of freedom to pursue her diverse interests. The cozy comfort of such a home will be like a calm, safe harbor and compensate for all of her vivaciousness, but she will have to look elsewhere for suggestions on deepening her pursuit of ideas and developing more serious interests. Now and then, things will also feel pretty boring.

But if we really want to help the sanguine child and do justice to her inner being, a degree of self-education is required of the adults—out of love for their child. If this is successful, the child will learn to overcome her weaknesses, and at the same time the parents will benefit greatly as they work on harmonizing their own temperaments. One becomes a sanguine person oneself along with one's sanguine child, and that means that of the four temperaments within, the parent learns to strengthen one that was previously underdeveloped. Not only the child, but the parent too has something to learn—what great motivation! We have already encountered this several times.

A further suggestion: Since sanguine children love to look at things (pictures, objects, people, animals, plants) but quickly lose interest, it is very important for them to gradually learn to observe important things more thoroughly and with concentration, for as long and continuously as possible. An example: An interesting picture with many small details is hanging on the wall—or we give it to the sanguine child to look at. We ask her to examine it very exactly and describe everything she sees. She will be able to discover and describe quite a few things that she really finds interesting. When she is convinced she has noticed *everything*, the parent can point out this or that detail, ask the child questions and direct her attention to all the other things still left to discover. If there are people in the picture, we could describe exactly what they're doing, what they're wearing, where exactly they are positioned, etc., so that our little observer notices all the things she overlooked. We could also ask her to notice all sorts of things in nature during a walk or other outdoor activity to sharpen her ability to observe.

It is probably easy to recognize that not only the sanguine child, but the adult as well, benefits from such exercises! We will need to summon the necessary inner composure and devote time to this. If we are encouraged to observe more exactly, we begin to develop new interests, and at the same time we learn to understand our child better. Through this further self-development, the adult has a stimulating effect on the self-education of the child, coming full circle.

Finally, Rudolf Steiner's suggestion should be mentioned here: It is very meaningful for sanguine children when the educator describes things about the world in a way that will really make an impression on them. Here it is important—even necessary—for the educator to add a little "spice," for example a humorous comment or aside. These are no doubt good for all listeners, but especially for the sanguine child's capacity to absorb what she hears! So it is understandable that boring descriptions are not only difficult for her to bear, but also heighten her distractibility.

The Phlegmatic Child

For phlegmatic children the rule also holds that similar things have a harmonious effect on each other. Therefore, if parents have a slow, deliberate child to deal with, a certain degree of calm and stability in the home is necessary. That is not a problem for parents with the same temperament, but it will not be easy for them to encourage the child to get interested in many things and give him advice and suggestions, since the parents themselves lack these qualities.

If a phlegmatic child grows up with strongly choleric parents, we can easily imagine him constantly being urged to hurry up and his parents getting aggravated because he does everything so slowly. Scolding, threatening, a little physical prodding, occasionally insulting or even ridiculing the child are not unusual, but they are all unfair toward this child's personality and, above all, wrongheaded: The child's phlegmatic tendencies will only be strengthened by treating him this way. He will more or less put on protective psychological "padding" in order to put up with everything.

If the child grows up in a home surrounded by people with strongly melancholic traits, he will generally receive a lot of attention, but such parents usually worry a lot: that he'll be late for school, that he daydreams too much and doesn't pay attention, that his grades aren't good enough, and so on. Such parents feel compelled to give their child constant orders, point out potential dangers, frequently ask him what he has learned, etc. But the more this happens, the more paralyzing an effect it can have on the phlegmatic child.

How different everything is if the sanguine temperament predominates at home: The upbeat atmosphere that radiates joy in life really does such children good. They receive all kinds of stimuli and ideas and interesting things are always happening, which will help him overcome the weaknesses of his temperament ("lack of interest" was what we termed the minor danger for this temperament).

The only way to help a phlegmatic child is to show a lot of understanding and trust his slow pace of development. One has to learn to be phlegmatic along with him. In this way, he can see himself reflected as in a mirror; he can recognize and educate himself. And what was said about the sanguine child holds true here, too: As educators we strengthen within ourselves a hitherto unnoticed temperament when we learn to activate our phlegmatic traits and, in so doing, acquire the grand characteristics of unflappability and tranquility.

If a phlegmatic child takes a long time to wake up in the morning and come to full consciousness, we should just wake him up earlier. This way he can do things at his own speed and doesn't need to be scolded or pressured. Rudolf Steiner also suggested that in some cases it is better to wash with cool instead of warm water, at least the face and hands, but if possible also the torso. This is refreshing and also wakes up the child. People have commented that this borders on asceticism, but I can only say that I learned to do this as a child and have continued ever since. Rudolf Steiner also suggested that phlegmatic children should not play with other phlegmatics after school, but rather with children who have lots of lively ideas and diverse interests, and will therefore have a stimulating effect.

The Choleric Child

We have already learned that choleric children want to feel respect for the adults raising and educating them; they want to look up to them, to admire what they are capable of achieving and how they behave. In other words, the choleric child highly regards people who are able to control themselves, who can serve as positive role models and cope successfully with things. She can look up to such people and learn the self-control that is so hard for her to develop. Such a child therefore places very high demands on her parents, too.

If the mother and father have a lot of choleric traits as well, on the one hand the child will see herself reflected, be able to unconsciously "wear down" her own strong temperament, and perhaps even get enthusiastic about many things she sees skillfully demonstrated. On the other hand, she will quickly lose respect if she experiences angry, uncontrolled outbursts from the people around her, because she'll see them as a weakness. After witnessing such an occurrence, it's not unusual for a choleric child

170

to react even more intensely or violently, or for family members to scream at, insult or even physically fight with one another.

If the parents have more phlegmatic traits, they will certainly stay much calmer when their child has a temper tantrum, but they may also act too indifferent or apathetic, and a choleric child may get even more upset if she has to experience this again and again. Woe betide anyone who smiles, much less pokes fun at this! And that counts for choleric adults as well.

Parents whose melancholic temperament is predominant will not tease or anger the child in the event of a temper tantrum; they will try to calm her down. If they have little understanding of their child's intense temperament, they may feel insulted and hurt by her offensive expressions and behavior. They may not forget it easily and even reproach her for it, delivering moralizing lectures, expressing their concerns, showing disapproval. As a result the child will suffer and, to find an outlet for her emotions, will let herself be provoked into reacting even more inappropriately or offensively.

Wherever the sanguine temperament dominates at home, parents generally treat their children kindly, don't let themselves be easily provoked, and are quick to respond with friendly words that they know will soothe a child's anger. But situations can also arise in which the choleric child doesn't feel she is being taken seriously, and when promises are made but not kept, she can easily get angry, resulting in an outburst. And heaven forbid that something should be unfairly divided up or distributed by such generous parents—that would be very hard for her to take!

From these few remarks about the significance of the temperaments at home, it should become clear that there is really no ideal combination. Of course, such situations can be depicted only in a schematic way; in individual cases we would discover a range of combinations and variations in the behavior of parents and children alike. Since difficulties can arise no matter what the constellation, self-education is a must.

With a choleric child, we need to learn to be choleric. This doesn't mean we should get angry along with her, since the tendency to react angrily is of course the minor danger of the choleric temperament; it must be replaced by the power of self-control. We must cultivate the ability to control ourselves and guide ourselves in the right direction. Anger is a fiery force within us, and we can control its flames! How rewarding when, out of love for a choleric child, we can learn to remold and reform our choleric strength so that our temperament does not control us, but we control our temperament. And what a boon for the child if she can grow up with such an example!

To deal with a choleric child, Steiner gave further suggestions: If she is not allowed to use up surplus energy by romping around and letting off steam, or is given no opportunities to use her arms and legs, the energy will get bottled up inside and make her restless. In this case we should give her a task requiring her to do something strenuous with her limbs.

Some teachers will quickly send a choleric child to the school office with a note before lessons begin in the morning if they notice that she is restless: "Run with this as fast as you can." Others will let such children run around the outside of the school building. Just as such a child is given particularly hard wood for carving a bowl so that she really has to use her muscles, she should be given difficult tasks and jobs at home that require particular strength. The world thus meets her with obstacles which are there to be mastered, and through which she can grow.

A further comment by Rudolf Steiner was not meant only jokingly, though it is hard not to smile: It is not wrong to allow choleric children to climb trees after school and let them shout at each other from up there. By doing both, they can use up their surplus energy.

Finally, Steiner repeatedly emphasized that one should demonstrate one's own talents to these children especially. How valuable for them if they discover and experience abilities in their father or mother that they themselves will be able to develop only through great effort and exertion. This will make all the difference, and will earn their parents great respect.

The Melancholic Child

As explained earlier, the melancholic child wants to feel that his educators are familiar with sorrow and grief and have experienced them personally. If the child comes to his mother or father to complain about something sad, we should seriously pay attention to this and put ourselves in the child's place. He is looking to be comforted, and we shouldn't fail him; but after that, it can be helpful to lovingly and tactfully tell him about even greater sorrow and troubles—something along the lines of the child whose notebook pages were willfully damaged by a classmate. His great capacity for sympathy will help him overcome his self-absorption and widen his horizons.

Parents with a predominantly melancholic temperament don't need any suggestions in this respect, since they have a great capacity to empathize with others, and a mutual reflecting or mirroring will take place at the same time. But hopefully there will also be lots to laugh about in such families, and they will know how to appreciate humor. It's actually not unusual for melancholics to have a very particular sense of humor, which we could describe as "dry." It has often been said that many a famous clown actually had a melancholic temperament.

It will also not be hard for sanguine parents to put themselves in their child's place, but only for a moment, so that even their subsequent comforting and consoling words may sound superficial. Thus it may happen that a melancholic child who seeks deeper contact and doesn't feel understood when he's left with his profoundly unfulfilled desires will eventually shut himself off—something that may even go unnoticed by the others. Nevertheless, the sunny sanguine disposition will generally have an agreeable effect.

Very phlegmatic fathers or mothers may show a certain indifference when their melancholic child comes running to them in tears yet again. They don't want to get worked up and cannot really imagine what it is like to have this amazingly deep temperament. All in all, the cozy, heartfelt atmosphere in a phlegmatic family will do the melancholic child good, but he will certainly have to look elsewhere for—and hopefully find—intellectual stimuli and a deep understanding of his innermost feelings.

Parents with a choleric temperament will generally show even less empathy for a melancholic child. They are constantly expected to show consideration for his many emotional and psychological nuances; they are constantly interrupted when the melancholic child comes with a grievance; they're expected to drop everything to listen to his woes, caused by somebody at school that day. That is just asking too much! "He shouldn't get so upset! You don't see me complaining – and how often would I have reason to! He comes and complains about every little thing!" If choleric parents react like this, it will certainly not help the melancholic. Some cholerics like to stand up for and protect others, and convey a feeling of security; and such a feeling of safety is what we would wish for the melancholic child.

The rule says we should learn to be melancholic with persons of melancholic temperament. What a great opportunity for mutual enrichment if parents would try to overcome their own temperament and, out of love for their child, assume a few of the impressive qualities of the melancholic temperament—such as becoming able to feel deeply and empathize profoundly.

Rudolf Steiner suggested that the teacher inwardly address the melancholic children when she asks for comments on previously taught material, and that the melancholics be asked more complicated, demanding questions. Parents can easily do this at home as well if they observe that the child likes to hold conversations with them. Appropriately for the child's age, one should talk to the melancholic child about many things, call his attention to details, prepare him for the realities of the world around him, and ask him questions. We should show great interest when speaking about aspects of the world, so that the child learns to open himself to the world.

Some melancholic children love it when their mother or father finds a few minutes' time in the evening to discuss this and that—preferably profound topics—even if only for five minutes. "Mama, can we have our five-minute talk again today?" said a child who was used to such frequent conversations.

As mentioned elsewhere, in adolescence melancholic children should read interesting biographies of great and important personalities, so they can experience what others have achieved and encountered, and in many cases endured or suffered through. Because they like to focus on their inner world, we need to show them the outer world. We should let them study detailed works of art as closely as possible. This will help them not to get lost in their own world, which is a definite possibility in adolescence.

To sum up, we can say that successful parenting involves not only dealing more skillfully with our children, but also includes the child's ability—as previously described for the teacher—to stimulate his or her parents to educate themselves, thus giving them the opportunity to develop further. If, after practicing this for a long time, we succeed in making this thought more and more an inner conviction, we will notice an entirely new relationship developing between us and our children, which will have a strong harmonizing effect.

The Temperaments and Nutrition

Every country and culture has its characteristic modes of nutrition. Every family, too, knows its own habits and exceptions. Nevertheless, let us venture to find at least two universally valid points of view for feeding children in accordance with their temperaments. Basic information on nutrition and many additional suggestions—also concerning the temperaments—can be found in Udo Renzenbrink's book *Ernährung unserer Kinder,*[17] which is the basis for the following explanations.

Four Kinds of Grain

All over the world, grain-based foods are staples of a healthy child's diet. So we can ask which kinds of grains have a connection to the four elements, and therefore also to the temperaments. From the many different grains that are cultivated, let us focus on the following four:

- rice, which is cultivated and consumed particularly in Asia
- millet, which originally came from Africa
- corn, which comes from the West, especially the Americas
- oats, which are cultivated worldwide.

If we look at how *rice* is grown, it immediately becomes clear that it always stands with its feet in water, and therefore has a connection to the water element.

If we look at *millet*, what strikes us are the tiny seeds in a very airy, panicle-like, multi-branched ear that can be blown back and forth by even a light breeze. The stalks are small and very finely structured, revealing that millet has a special connection to the air element.

Corn, on the other hand, is a very strong plant with a thick, fleshy stalk surrounded by long, deep green leaves. In contrast to all other kinds of grain, the fruit, the corn cob, grows farther down the stalk and is wrapped in a leaflike husk. The golden, sweetish kernels of corn ripen inside in darkness and look like small cubes. Here we are dealing with the earth element.

Oats, which are known for their use as concentrated feed for horses, are connected to the fire element. They do not grow very tall, stretch their stalks as high as they can and feature a separate sheath for each seed, which grows on its own stalk so it can stretch toward the sun and absorb its warmth.

By recognizing the connections of these four grains to the elements, we also have the key to the corresponding temperament: The law that "like cures like" applies here.

Rice has a harmonizing effect on the phlegmatic person, but we can also stimulate his consciousness by strongly seasoning the rice—it can get very hot and spicy (for example, with curry)! In general, phlegmatic children enjoy eating and eat a lot, so we must be careful to limit portions at meals to keep them from becoming overweight.

With its cheery, tiny little seeds, millet is the grain for the sanguine personality. It undoubtedly requires a certain degree of cooking talent to make this relatively unknown food tasty and to develop a variety of recipes, since the sanguine child needs to like what she sees in order to enjoy eating it. And she really loves it when the food on her plate looks interesting. We should garnish our meals colorfully, because this will improve the sanguine child's appetite—something she needs, since she is not a "good eater." Parents should not be concerned if only relatively little food is sometimes eaten; sanguine children do not need much. They also consume a lot of sense impressions and get full quickly. For preparing grains there are now countless cookbooks full of interesting and delicious recipes, including ones devoted to millet.

The grain of the melancholic is corn, with its fairly sweet flavor. There are many ways to prepare delicious corn dishes. It isn't easy to tempt melancholic children with food; they are very picky and frequently not hungry, so they, too, are not "good eaters." Since they need a lot of warmth, it's good to feed them a lot of cooked foods, and not too many raw fruits and vegetables: these require a lot of inner warmth to digest, which the body will then miss.

The choleric grain is oats. Oats provide a lot of energy and strength, but at the same time have a harmonizing effect through the principle of "mirroring." Choleric children have a lot of heat of their own that sometimes gets the better of them, so we can easily feed them raw fruits and vegetables, which they will use their inner warmth to digest. The choleric child is a "good eater," loves hearty, substantial meals and manages to eat large portions.

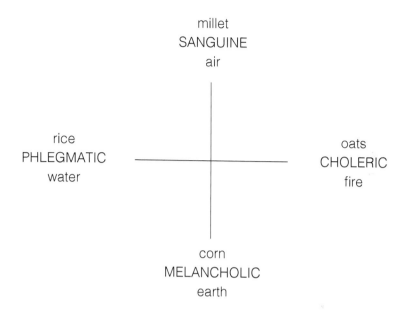

Of course, all these suggestions aren't always easy to put into everyday practice. What should parents cook if they have several children with different temperaments? What should we do if our child won't eat the grain associated with his/her temperament?

We may only sporadically have the opportunity to influence a temperament by cooking the appropriate grain, so we shouldn't worry about this too much. Since we want to look at all aspects of the temperaments, these suggestions for nutrition can be optional, and it is left to the free initiative of readers whether or not to follow them. A parent can only put something into practice if it is done voluntarily and in a sensible, natural way for the child.

Sugar and the Temperaments

The following suggestion by Rudolf Steiner is especially important for melancholic and sanguine children, and is relatively easy to put into practice. It has to do with sugar: Steiner recommends giving the melancholic child a bit more and the sanguine child a bit less. Let's examine why, and take a look at a simple example that will make it clear.

It is common knowledge that through complicated processes of digestion, our body converts all foods that we consume into a certain form of sugar and then releases it into the bloodstream, where it is referred to as "blood sugar." We can already perceive something of this sugar process if we put a small piece of bread in our mouth and chew it for a few minutes: We notice a sweet taste. (If you have never tried this, you should really do so once.) So if we take in sugar from outside, our body has to make less of an effort, and the soul and spirit qualities subconsciously connected with this process lose a bit of their hold over the body and exert less of an influence on it. If, on the other hand, we consume less sugar, our body becomes more active and has to raise the blood sugar level on its own. This occurs through the functioning of the liver, which regulates the storing and breaking down of glycogen to affect blood sugar levels.

The sanguine person usually has a somewhat looser connection with her physical body, while the melancholic person has a somewhat tighter connection. From daily life we know that people who are having difficulties—perhaps even love problems—unconsciously turn to sweets, especially chocolate. The sugar does indeed help us cope with our problems, because it has a relaxing effect that helps to free our soul and spirit qualities from the heaviness of the physical body.

For the sanguine temperament, too much sugar makes one uneasy, even fidgety and restless. Of course it's precisely people with this temperament who love sweets and are intrigued by colorful candy treats; they will happily give in to temptation. Here parents are confronted with a difficult task, but making the effort is really worth it.

Rudolf Steiner suggested that a mother should gradually attempt—in small steps from week to week—to reduce her sanguine child's daily intake of sugar. For example, if a child is used to drinking tea with three teaspoonfuls of sugar, one should reduce this to two and a half the first week, then only two, then even less until a much lower amount is reached—or none at all! According to this principle in reverse, one would gradually add sugar to a melancholic child's tea in the course of the next few weeks and tactfully try to find an acceptable limit. In both cases, we should not tell the child anything about the reason.

It is obvious that the sugar industry's tempting offerings of colorful candy are detrimental to children's development, especially so for sanguines, who are attracted to bright colors. For years it has been well known and addressed in countless publications that a correlation exists between hyperactivity in children and their consumption of food additives and high-phosphate snacks, including most kinds of candy. (In Germany they are even referred to as "phosphate kids," but there have been absolutely no consequences either in the sugar industry or on the pedagogical side.) Rudolf Steiner's suggestion confirms these facts and provides us with a stimulus to act responsibly.

Since all children are somewhat sanguine compared to adults, what has been said here actually holds true for all children, regardless of their dominant temperament.

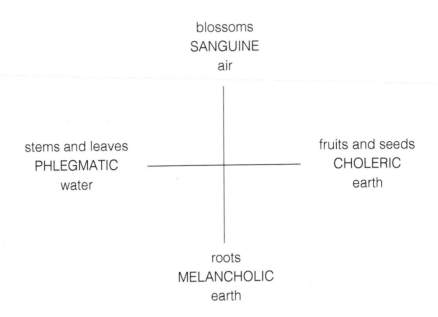

blossoms
SANGUINE
air

stems and leaves
PHLEGMATIC
water

fruits and seeds
CHOLERIC
earth

roots
MELANCHOLIC
earth

The Four Parts of the Plant and Nutrition

Finally, let us make some observations regarding the consumption of plants. Naturally, we will feed our children all the different parts of a plant, but it may be interesting to learn that certain parts have a special relationship to one element, and therefore to one of the temperaments. I refer here again to the suggestions made by Udo Renzenbrink.[18]

Let us begin with the root of a plant. What interesting kinds of roots—of all sorts of different colors—exist worldwide and find their way to our dinner table! They have a close connection to the earth element and thus with the melancholic person.

All the vegetables whose stems or leaves we eat are particularly suited to phlegmatic children. We have already associated this part of the plant with the water element.

Through their relationship with the air, blossoms with all their beautiful colors and aromas have a harmonizing effect on the sanguine child. Here the various blossom teas come to mind, which appeal to the senses not only with their colors but also with their fragrances.

Fruit and seeds ripened in the sun are really important foods for all children, but because of their relationship with the element of warmth, they are particularly good for choleric children. Nuts belong to this group. Rudolf Steiner said that every schoolchild should eat a few nuts every day because they will help children concentrate better. And that, too, is good for choleric children!

The Effect of Colors

It is common knowledge that colors have certain effects on people; accordingly, colors are used for their psychological impact in various industries. Goethe already spoke about the sensory-moral effects of the different colors. From the stoplights at traffic intersections, we know that red was intentionally selected to mean "stop" because it is a very active color, has an awakening effect and advances toward the observer, whereas the color blue recedes or withdraws. A room with red wallpaper appears smaller; one with blue walls seems larger. Color therapy in which patients are exposed to colored light has had astonishingly successful results.

Rudolf Steiner mentioned the possibility of using certain colors in accordance with the temperaments for children's immediate surroundings. We know that for every color we see and take in, our eye creates the complementary color. By way of experiments in physics class, the children learn this as the law of complementary colors.

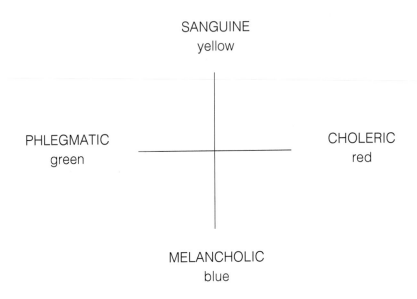

SANGUINE
yellow

PHLEGMATIC
green

CHOLERIC
red

MELANCHOLIC
blue

We can guess that choleric children not only love red, but are also positively influenced by this color. If we look at a patch of red for a minute, we will soon see green before our eyes. It is this green that has a calming effect on a choleric child, which is a very significant fact.

Taking a walk in the woods has an especially refreshing effect. We see green all around us, and our eye therefore creates an activating red. For a phlegmatic person, the green tones are therefore particularly important.

The sanguine child should be surrounded by as many yellow things as possible, because yellow makes the eye produce the complementary color, violet—a color that helps sanguine children concentrate and internalize their focus.

And for the melancholic child it is blue, which is internalized as orange: an activating, brightening color.

There are many possible ways to use these colors in children's surroundings. The most obvious is to paint the bedroom walls the appropriate color. If we do so, we should apply the paint not in a thick layer, but in a way that lets the color stay translucent: We mix a very thin solution of the paint and apply it with a sponge using circular or curving strokes, then apply another layer the same way—and after it has dried, yet another layer. This technique is called "glazing" or "lazuring." It lets the color "breathe" and greatly contributes to harmonizing children's temperaments.

Note: Colors do not necessarily have the same effects on the temperaments of adults. Red, for example, would not have a calming effect on a choleric adult, but might well foster aggression instead.

10. The Temperaments in Adult Relationships

What to Look Out For

In the course of our study we have encountered the unique positive attributes of the individual temperaments, as well as learning about their negative sides. Now we'll take another look at the temperaments, this time with regard to the basics of living with siblings, parents or relatives, or when cultivating a friendship or intimate relationship. At the same time we will examine how we might behave when our partner does not succeed in curbing or controlling his/her temperament. Hopefully, it will become clear that many a difficulty in life can be more easily overcome—or even avoided—if we understand something about this topic.

Let's now try to imagine the different effects each temperament might have on another, and what we should watch out for. We will need to keep in mind that most people have at least two active temperaments, and that the other two may put in an appearance as well, under certain circumstances. We should also remember that the temperaments represent only one aspect of a human being, and that individual cases will differ greatly. So the following descriptions will not, and do not claim to, provide adequate explanations for all possible behavior patterns. They are intended as a general guide.

Choleric and Phlegmatic

Since experience shows that it is the choleric temperament that causes the most difficulties in social situations, we will deal with it in some detail.

We have come to know choleric and phlegmatic individuals as distinct opposites, which also holds true when they are living together. It is truly great and admirable to observe how a choleric contemplates and sets her sights on new goals and, ready for action, figures out how to accomplish them! She likes phlegmatics because she can rely on them and because they are always good-natured and exude pleasantness, as well as a sense of calm she herself is not capable of achieving easily. Phlegmatic people have many qualities that she lacks, and she appreciates and respects this. But if she constantly has to watch her phlegmatic partner behaving so differently, taking forever to do anything, approaching every task deliberately, making things much too cozy and comfortable and wanting them to stay that way, it will be hard for her to be understanding. She'll explode with angry, cutting words or even fly into a rage as she tries to get him going. After she calms down, she will probably be astounded that her phlegmatic partner didn't take offense at her thoughtless insults, that he always excuses her short temper and never complains about it or holds any of it against her. (Maybe, deep inside, the phlegmatic is even grateful to her, although he doesn't show it.)

For his part, the phlegmatic person experiences many qualities in the choleric that he himself does not possess but really admires. He is really fond of her, he can learn a lot from her, and he knows she just needs to let off steam every once in a while. He cannot and does not want to get upset about it; he manages to stay calm and not lose his temper. But this is exactly what can really get on the choleric's nerves! Oh, how she would love just once to shake him out of his lethargic state and have a real heated argument! But it just doesn't work—and that makes her angry! The phlegmatic partner knows from experience that the storm will soon pass, and that it's better not to infuriate his friend by smiling. He just needs to keep quiet and wait for the storm or volcanic eruption to be over.

It is particularly difficult for the phlegmatic to change himself—but this is also true for the choleric, who will be able to endure being at his side for any length of time only if she can develop some understanding of his placid and very likeable temperament.

Choleric and Melancholic

The nobler aspects of the melancholic personality can be very impressive to our choleric firebrand: an exceptional capacity for clear, logical thinking; seriousness and depth; inner composure, deep empathy and loyalty are all qualities that she greatly admires. The melancholic, in turn, also appreciates all the pluses of the choleric temperament. But he also has the tendency to criticize and complain, which the choleric easily finds fault with and finds very annoying. If she starts yelling and swearing and calling him names, the melancholic will tend to withdraw inwardly and remain silent. After her anger is gone, she probably won't remember what she said and expects life to go on as usual, but that isn't so easy for the melancholic. He feels shocked and hurt, broods over why his dear friend said such terrible things about him, and will need some time to get over it. He also knows he will never be able to forget her insults.

Meanwhile our choleric no longer knows what she said in anger, remembers only that she was releasing the pressure inside her, and now considers herself completely in the right. The next day, however, her guilty conscience bothers her, and she wants to make up for everything. At that point it is a good idea for the melancholic partner, with his strong intellectual abilities, to come to the realization that yesterday's outburst was just like a natural phenomenon, a volcanic eruption. Of course we wouldn't reproach a volcano for erupting, and we know it will probably erupt again. Nevertheless, we do need to speak to our choleric friend about what happened so she can become increasingly aware of the effects of her actions. But how to do that?

When we discussed how a teacher should react to a choleric child's fit of rage, we made some basic points; we will need to modify these somewhat when dealing with adults, and also keep all the temperaments in mind. As an example, let us assume that our choleric partner loses her temper, yells and curses and calls us nasty names to our face. Maybe she even throws things or intentionally damages things. What should we do?

It is usually pointless to attempt a thorough discussion immediately afterward, or even for the next few hours; it's best to wait for the next day, if we can muster the courage and patience.

However, immediately after the incident we do need to do as follows, or else our choleric friend will not be able to recall the incident and how she acted. During (or right after) the tantrum, we must point out what she has said or done. This can be expressed as an impartial question: "Was it necessary for you to smash the vase (plate, cup...) on the floor?" Or: "Did you have to call me an idiot?" In might take courage to do this, but the question will wake the choleric up. She is really not conscious of what happened: She experiences episodes like her intense fit of anger as a brief state of sleep, which is why she will absolutely not remember it, try as she may.

Under no circumstances should we hurl insults back at the choleric. She will never be able to ignore or forget that, and it will just magnify her anger. She will get so upset that she'll never be able to talk about it the next day in a friendly but direct conversation.

It is well known that a choleric partner frequently has a guilty conscience the next day and try to compensate by bringing home a special gift, offering to help, or being particularly friendly and remorseful. The conversation we have with them should not have a moralizing tone; it should be objective and have the purpose of bringing clarity to the situation. The melancholic (or anyone else who has gone through such an experience with a choleric) should also point out the effect it had on him, and the position he was put into as a result of her behavior. If our choleric friend then apologizes and promises not to do it again, the melancholic partner should keep in mind that she sincerely means it and wants to keep her promise... but that she will probably hit the roof again sometime in the future.

If a number of these conversations and subsequent apologies have taken place over the course of several years together, we might be tempted to say, "You've already apologized ten times, so why should I believe you this time?" We should be aware that this will only insult our choleric friend, and may even provoke another fit of anger.

Living together is not very easy for these two temperaments, but if they both have the necessary understanding for each other, it can be successful.

Choleric and Sanguine

A sanguine person easily gets enthusiastic. In a choleric friend she may discover many qualities that she admires, finds interesting and cannot imitate herself. The fact that her friend is always getting worked up about things and flying into a rage she finds less pleasant, but in such situations she is usually able to react diplomatically and knows what to do to hopefully defuse the situation and stop an argument from developing. She tries to avoid that. She also doesn't hold it against him if he lets off steam once in a while or gets into a bad mood because she, with her merry, carefree nature, does things too quickly and incompletely; her feelings are not immediately hurt, nor does she feel insulted. She is able to think of a few friendly, helpful words to tame his anger and not add fuel to the fire. But if her choleric partner treats her badly and puts a complete damper on life with constant reproaches and insults, her sanguine nature will seek out new and positive experiences by meeting other people, having a good time and fanning her ego and self-esteem in the process.

For the choleric person, it is a great pleasure to be with such a fun, cheerful partner who always has good ideas, radiates enthusiasm, is quick and active, and has a wide range of interests. But there are a number of things that he objects to and has trouble putting up with. He—who when he begins something can find no peace until it is finished—is incensed by the fact that she likes to start things but quickly loses interest, loves to party and celebrate, preferably with lots of people, is always buying new clothes and never worries about how much she's spending. No— when he compares this behavior to his own, the choleric has a hard time accepting it. Something must be done to stop this! He cannot empathize with such behavior—as we saw in the choleric reactions to a phlegmatic or melancholic partner. He is, of course, very sure of himself: It's his way or the highway!

Despite all this, we can often observe choleric-sanguine partnerships getting along quite well, as long as they don't lose their mutual respect and their verbal sparring doesn't get out of hand. To a large extent, that depends on whether the sanguine partner's ability to love is great enough, and whether their inner connection is strong enough to overcome all the potential difficulties.

Choleric and Choleric

It is actually not unusual for two cholerics to team up and form a partnership. As they get to know one another, they each discover a quality or ability in the other that they really admire. Now that is something that really commands my respect! That is something special that I can't do myself! I would really love to learn how to do it and – if possible –do it even better! That is a great motivator: a choleric's ambition.

At the same time, they are both looking into a mirror and seeing themselves, though they do not want to admit it. That can easily lead to friction and quarrels. They each have their own position, they each know better than the other and want their partner to finally realize this and give in. They accuse each other of making the same mistakes and are soon upset, angry and ultimately furious! They blame each other for picking a fight again, starting again with the same old annoying issues, and always wanting to be right. They raise their voices, yell at each other, and then at some point both have had enough and calm down; they come back to their senses, confess how much they love each other and can't imagine being apart—and vow to do better in the future. Then they celebrate their reconciliation, laugh about it, and all is forgotten—until next time!

When we turn to the other possible combinations in relationships, we will see that in some cases the essentials can be summed up in a few words.

Phlegmatic and Melancholic

We can imagine that if we put a phlegmatic together with a melancholic, peace will predominate. The melancholic admires the tranquility of his quiet partner; he thought it over carefully before finally making the decision to move in with her. He knows that he can rely on her and that she will be faithful to him. Add to that the feelings of warmth and satisfaction that she so loves and emanates—no rush, no prickly remarks, always affable, and she doesn't get offended when he corrects her or urges her to do things faster.

At their very first meeting, the phlegmatic sensed that she feels good with this person, that he thinks deeply about things, knows a lot and is very empathetic and honest. However, she did not imagine a steady relationship for a long time, nor did she notice that her companion was waiting for a declaration of love.

And she had no idea what to say in such a situation. Up to then, she had had no interest in such a relationship, but now she feels good about things and finds nothing to object to in her partner.

One thing, though, does bother her and is beginning to make her feel a bit dissatisfied: For a while now he has been pointing out things she could have done better. She should be more organized; she should take less time to get ready when they go out at night; it would be good if she read the papers regularly so she would know what's happening in the world. In the meantime the melancholic has also discovered that our phlegmatic is not really interested in a lot of things; she likes best to sit in front of the TV, though she watches only certain programs, and she doesn't read any more— it's too much work. He thinks it would be great to go to the opera, a play or a classical concert once in a while, but it doesn't happen due to lack of interest. How often he has suggested good ideas for things they could do together, but it has all been in vain.

But the phlegmatic person cannot understand why her partner always has to moan and groan about things. Life could be so pleasant! Food always tastes good, and her partner does enjoy a glass of wine—and in the company of others, more than one glass; if they are at a party and he's having a good time, he finds it hard to leave. But these are all things she dislikes. She is no friend of parties, which she considers too superficial.

Thus we see that it's not easy for a melancholic person if his partner has few interests. So he should start out early on to try to make the outside world, with all its beautiful and interesting features, tempting to his phlegmatic friend, and motivate her to come along. For after a certain point in time he will no longer be able to achieve this; the phlegmatic person will have grown too accustomed to the status quo. We must also remember that, while it is easy to constantly reproach a phlegmatic person, endless criticism will paralyze her emotionally, make her listless and force her to feel that, despite all her efforts, she can never do anything to satisfy her partner. In this situation she will grow even more phlegmatic in order to be able to bear it. As is generally known, we speak of "worry weight," the excess weight people put on due to emotional problems, and our phlegmatic friends are already prone to gaining weight.

Those of us with a phlegmatic temperament should therefore learn early on to keep our weight under control and otherwise learn to pull ourselves together and, out of love for our partners, make their interests our own. We should also make sure we get enough exercise. Doing things together such as taking walks and hikes, playing sports (melancholics and phlegmatics will both be good sports), and sharing common intellectual interests are all very important in contributing to a harmonious life.

Phlegmatic and Sanguine

As a rule, a phlegmatic person shows goodwill toward a sanguine, is delighted by her jokes, likes to laugh at them, and is amazed at her many ideas, her quick actions and her ability to react. Many of these are things he would also like to be able to do, but he is content with the way he is. He likes to listen to the sanguine talking as long as the topic interests him, but if she jumps from one subject to another and is always talking about something new, the phlegmatic cannot and will not follow what she is saying. He will just sit there quietly, without criticizing. He accepts his fellow human beings the way they are and would like to be treated accordingly.

The sanguine person also likes her phlegmatic friend: He is so easy-going, never starts an argument, is never rude or pushy, and is quiet and modest. Yes, sometimes she'd even like to be that quiet for a change! If she—who is so enterprising and wants to get to know the world from all sides and see lots of things—expects her phlegmatic friend to participate in all sorts of activities, she is quite mistaken. She will have to make things happen on her own while he stays home, happy that his "whirlwind" friend has allowed him some peace and quiet for a change.

Both these temperaments have a predisposition for mutual tolerance and will get along very well, as long as the sanguine does not pick up a new companion during her excursions into the world. So we should encourage phlegmatics to join their sanguine partners and let themselves be stimulated to find new interests as often as possible—comparable to the way we described for school children.

For the sanguine partner, the calm composure of the phlegmatic is also a great relief, like a peaceful haven she returns to after a storm. But since she is unable to imitate his qualities easily, they remain a far distant goal that she will be able to achieve only after much work on herself.

Phlegmatic and Phlegmatic

When two cholerics are together, they don't cope well with seeing their own temperament mirrored in the other, and as adults they don't unconsciously "wear down" each other's temperament as children do. In fact, the opposite might happen: In many cases their tendency, which we described as a quick temper, is strengthened instead. We discover the same principle when two phlegmatics live together: They won't make each other more conscious or active; usually the opposite happens. Neither one will disapprove if the other likes to relax and take it easy, sleep late, eat a lot, reduce the scope of his or her interests more and more, and noticeably put on the pounds. But it need not come to this if one of the two nurtures some outside interests, including intellectual ones; likes to exercise; pays attention to portion sizes; and understands how to motivate the other to do the same.

Actually, as a consequence of unhealthy diets, the decrease in physical movement and the proliferation of electronic devices, on-demand movies, video games, etc., adults and children worldwide are gaining more and more weight and becoming increasingly sluggish, idle and lethargic. In short, they are becoming more and more phlegmatic, though this may not be their dominant temperament—but since we all have all four temperaments within us, such a shift is entirely possible.

Rudolf Steiner expressed deep concern to teachers, advising them to take care that children do not gain too much weight, because then their spiritual and intellectual powers and abilities will not be able to develop correctly.

To summarize, then, we can say that phlegmatic partners get along very well, live together peacefully and comfortably, develop few interests and have to pay close attention to maintaining a healthy diet and getting enough exercise.

Sanguine and Melancholic

Now let us observe how a very happy temperament tries to live life at the side of a very serious one. What a great contrast—yet it is not unusual for them to feel strongly attracted to each other!

Our sanguine subject discovers all the things in her melancholic partner that she lacks emotionally and is not capable of, and she admires and loves his inner depth, earnestness, preciseness and inscrutability. She can depend on the melancholic; she knows he will remain faithful to her because it took him a long time to be ready to reveal his innermost feelings to her. Our sanguine friend was also immediately impressed by his intellectual interests, and intends to take them up herself—at least, that is what she vowed to do at once!

The melancholic personality is a very good and keen observer. Through his sanguine partner he often recognizes that he does not possess her admirable abilities and qualities, and—at least at the beginning of their relationship—he experiences so much joy with her: She is so cheerful and upbeat, she loves to laugh, knows how to make him laugh and has such a confident manner when they go to parties. She knows so many different people; everyone likes her; she even approaches complete strangers and can start conversing with them as if she has known them her whole life. That she can do all those things! No, there is no possible way he could do that! Two completely different worlds meet.

But the melancholic doesn't like to go to such social events where people just want to celebrate, dance, drink, laugh and have a good time. His partner loves them, but as far as he is concerned, there aren't enough suitable people to talk to—people he can converse with seriously. And he already knows in advance that our sanguine friend loves to dance and flirt with everyone, which is also a reason why he would prefer not to go. But letting his companion go alone is also no solution.

If we try to slip into his shoes, we can understand not only his indecision, but also the fact that he often manages to avoid such events by "getting sick" or coming down with some disorder that will prevent him from going out. In this way, he "has to, unfortunately," stay home, which spoils the sanguine partner's pleasant anticipation, and if this happens too often, eventually robs her of her *joie de vivre*. The evening could have been so much fun, and think of all the people she would have seen there! Our sanguine friend, who would, of course, like to please everyone, especially her melancholic partner, is strongly influenced by his moods and is happy when he's happy. But if she is criticized frequently despite all her efforts to improve, and reminded of small faults such as being messy, late, superficial or careless, her self-confidence will sink more and more, and living with her partner can become a real struggle. If only she could satisfy him! If she doesn't succeed, she will seek the acknowledgment she needs from other people who like her and are nice to her. She herself feels no need to criticize her companion, and if she does happen to do so, she always feels guilty because she senses that she is constantly making so many mistakes that she really has no justification for complaining.

Let us make a recommendation to all those who are melancholic. In horse racing there is an expression that applies to dealing with sanguines: "Wild horses should be kept on a long lead." They can be tamed only in this way, not by keeping them tightly confined. And a seafarer's expression says something very comforting about temporary separations: "A good sailor who has traveled afar always loves to return to his native harbor—the one he calls home!" Similarly, our melancholic friend should allow his sanguine companion plenty of freedom of movement and provide her with a home that she will always like to return to after her "voyages," because that's where she feels best and hopefully also most deeply loved.

Sanguine and Sanguine

Wow, this is a meeting of two happy-go-lucky characters! We'll see that here, too, everything holds true that we have said about the common ground between two similar temperaments—at least if one of them isn't a mixture that counteracts the union.

They happily approach each other, spontaneously like each other, approve of the other person's interests and adopt them for themselves, enjoy getting together with other people and making a lot of new friends. They love a bit of variety and constantly need new impressions—interesting novelty. Wherever they are, there's a lot going on, and in the hustle and bustle they get along perfectly and feel right at home. They both love to joke and kid around, to entertain others and tell the latest gossip, and it is easy to imagine them competing with each other to be the first to tell their friends the breaking news. And we can sense how this all contributes to strengthening their sanguine qualities.

Neither likes to be alone, and when they are home together, it doesn't take them long to report all the latest news. Since it is uninteresting to kid around and tell each other jokes they both already know, they're constantly on the lookout for new diversions, which they will definitely discover. They may plan big things and really look forward to experiencing them together— but sometimes they just turn out to be castles in the air, unless one of the two is more of a realist.

Since both of them are quite lovable, it of course happens that they meet people with whom they immediately fall in love and devote all their attention to. This will be completely unexpected for the partner, but generally it will last only a short time. If it should lead to a breakup, the affected partner will know how to drown his or her sorrows and find consolation, namely the same way. They will both tend to promise their companions to be faithful, and have a hard time keeping the promise. But we must emphasize that all sanguines love so many people so intensely during their lifetimes that they are extremely saddened and depressed for a long time when they lose a partner to a breakup or death.

Both sanguine partners see themselves reflected in the other, who becomes a mirror, presenting a subconscious opportunity for self-knowledge. This can help the partners take the necessary steps, if they make a great effort and if they really want to... but they like life much better without having to deal with steps to self-knowledge.

Melancholic and Melancholic

Two people get together who take life seriously, think about everything, observe life critically and like to discuss deep, intellectually stimulating topics. Together they lead a very conscious life, agreeing on interests each will pursue separately and those they can pursue together, and allowing each other ample personal space to be alone without offending the other. There is a clear order to everything; life is discussed and planned out with precision.

After living together for a while, the two know each other very well and although they see themselves mirrored in each other, they resist seeing it in case one of them is incapable of being self-critical. From then on, many a trait in the partner can be found fault with. Mutual criticism begins; suggestions for improving the relationship are made; one of the two suddenly feels ill, hoping to win the other's sympathy, but the other has something bothering her too, and so on.

We see in this combination, too, that the same temperaments in adults do not automatically harmonize; rather, they intensify in the absence of self-criticism. Compared with the others, the melancholic is most likely to be self-critical, so he is always a bit dissatisfied with himself. But this is a long way from practicing true self-criticism, which requires strong willpower.

There is a well-known saying: "Opposites attract." That is true, but what is meant is that people with similar interests like to get together and pursue them. But when two similar temperaments get together, a sort of mirroring takes place as well, which challenges both of the "kindred spirits" with a task to be fulfilled.

The Significance of the Temperaments in Social Life

Up to now we have observed each of the temperaments by itself, and then imagined how two of them affect each other in relationship. Now we will try to see all four in connection with each other, and ask ourselves what significance we can ascribe to them in social life and what purposes they may have. We can determine this by looking at the valuable qualities each possesses. The best way to illustrate this is by using an example: the founding of a Waldorf school and the furnishing of the new school building.

All around the globe, Waldorf schools come into being because of parents' heartfelt mission of creating such a school for their children. Government assistance can be counted on almost nowhere, so practically everything depends on the initiative of a few people who take the first steps. This requires courage, determination, drive and persistence. These are the character traits of the choleric personality! The choleric must motivate and urge on the others, and give them the feeling that this project is absolutely achievable!

The sanguine parents joyfully agree, get really enthusiastic and have lots of ideas for finding more potentially interested parents. They spread the word to many others, promote the idea wherever they can and make sure to meet regularly. Speeches will have to be made by experienced Waldorf teachers, who must be identified, invited, scheduled, perhaps picked up at the train or airport, taken care of when they arrive, etc. Who could do this better than the sanguine parents? However, everything will need to be well planned and thought through.

Many things don't work as easily and simply as we first thought. "Shouldn't we go over the details again just to be sure? Shouldn't we form an official association and elect board members, including a treasurer to be in charge of the finances? Who will volunteer for this time-consuming job? Where should the school be situated? Where can we find teachers? Where can they go for training? Won't we need a permit or a license from the state?" Who else worries about such things? Here we can rely on the strong points of the melancholic personality.

"It will all work out fine. Just stay calm, ladies and gentlemen. One step at a time, let's not get ahead of ourselves. We should also get together sometime to celebrate over dinner – nothing too formal. We could get to know and understand each other better that way," we hear our phlegmatic friend say. And she is right: Doing something together, especially eating a common meal, connects people. But the phlegmatics don't only create a pleasant atmosphere, spread oil on the waters and model persistence and perseverance; they are also willing and able to take responsibility, for example as treasurer, for they work carefully and conscientiously. They are natural bookkeepers who won't despair if a mistake is made. When occasional arguments arise, the phlegmatic's peace-loving, friendly personality usually comes in handy.

This is how things might look at the beginning of the founding of a school. Let us now observe the roles the different temperaments play at a later point: planning and furnishing the school building. Parents and teachers need to decide on what color to paint the classrooms and need to work on the floors, the shelves and cupboards, to lay out the playground, etc.

For these jobs they usually meet on weekends. The choleric parents lend an energetic hand and gladly take on difficult physical tasks—especially ones whose results can be seen and shown afterward. They work diligently like skilled manual laborers and don't quit until everything is done! They like to be seen as doing their jobs especially well, and place great importance on having their work acknowledged by others. And justifiably so, for who else could do the hard, dirty work on the building as exactly and masterfully as they have?

The sanguine parents always know how to keep busy and like to take on simpler, easier, more varied jobs that they can do in the company of other people while carrying on lively conversations. Wherever they are, there will be jokes, laughter and a happy mood. They'll gladly interrupt their work to walk around and see what the others are doing, and they're delighted to meet other future school parents this way. If their work is not done perfectly, it does not bother them. If there is any grumbling about it, it can come only from the choleric parents.

Melancholic adults with their thorough attention to detail are also needed when building a school, especially where accuracy is important, for example when painting and installing molding and baseboards or laying electric wiring. They will always be critical observers and advisors who occasionally point out where something needs to be done much more carefully. They don't like to take on physical tasks like carrying heavy beams or boards, and because of their often fragile physiques, such tasks should not necessarily be expected of them.

The phlegmatic parents will not complain if they have to do jobs that other people—like the sanguines—aren't interested in because they sound so boring: painting the basement walls white, cutting countless pieces of molding to a certain length, planting the flower beds. Once they have started, they will do their work calmly and conscientiously, perhaps taking short breaks every once in a while, and generally staying in good spirits. If asked to carry something heavy, they will gladly contribute their physical strength for the common good. And if an argument starts anywhere, their peacemaking qualities can be very helpful.

Let us consider this description to be an example showing how each temperament is needed in its own way in society. Taken all together they form a unified whole, and none of them should be missing! They all need each other.

11. Self-Education

What Do We Need to Learn?

Before we turn to the important question of what each of us can do to control and master our main temperament—instead of letting ourselves be controlled by it, so that it can do with us as it pleases—let us shed light on the talents and shortcomings of each of the four temperaments another way.

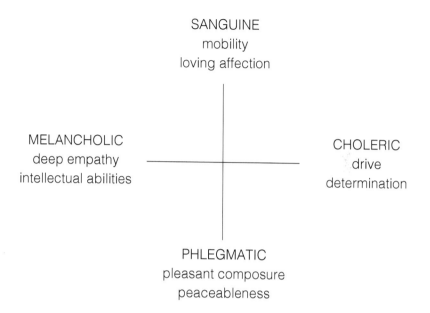

SANGUINE
mobility
loving affection

MELANCHOLIC
deep empathy
intellectual abilities

CHOLERIC
drive
determination

PHLEGMATIC
pleasant composure
peaceableness

The choleric is skilled at putting his will into action with his limbs, but he lacks self-control and often intellectual clarity. The melancholic is the good thinker who likes to work with her head but is not easily roused to action. Seen in this way, she contrasts with the choleric. The sanguine is characterized by the gifts of great mobility and loving affection, but lacks the strength to persevere and rest. In contrast to the sanguine, the phlegmatic radiates pleasant calmness but lacks mobility and excitability.

Gerda Scheer-Krüger has pointed out many further valuable aspects of the temperaments,[19] and I would like to refer to some of the shortcomings she mentions.

To begin with, let us place the talents and shortcomings opposite each other. This time, the temperaments are in different positions. We will later discover that this is a good preparation for our suggestions for self-education.

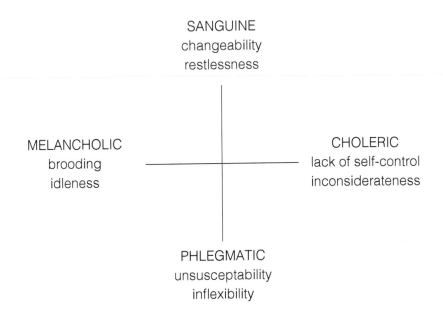

SANGUINE
changeability
restlessness

MELANCHOLIC
brooding
idleness

CHOLERIC
lack of self-control
inconsiderateness

PHLEGMATIC
unsusceptability
inflexibility

How Our Temperaments Affect Children

The task of working on our own temperament, which constantly threatens to slip out of our grasp and control us, becomes even more urgent when we look at how uncontrolled outbreaks of temperament can affect our children, our students and our fellow human beings.

If we imagine a child growing up in a family where a parent flies into a rage nearly every day, yells, blames others for everything and sometimes even falsely accuses the child, it is obvious that this behavior will have dire consequences for the child over time. It will first affect her emotional and mental balance, then increasingly her health and well-being. The fact that fear, horror and shock have consequences is obvious to any of us who have had to experience this, and psychosomatic medicine confirms that one's health can be severely affected. If a teacher or family member suddenly gets loud, violent and out of control, he will shock a child whether he intends to or not.

A very phlegmatic adult would not act that way toward children. But what are the effects of the extreme form of the phlegmatic temperament on a child living in close proximity? A certain degree of apathy in a parent or teacher might be welcome these days: Such a person will remain calm and composed, won't get easily upset or violent, and will always use a calm teaching voice. But if her phlegmatic temperament gets too intense and is allowed to develop to excess, she will not be sufficiently receptive to the children's various interests and questions. There will be too many things she simply ignores or doesn't care about, and the children will feel as if they were breathing "thin air." They will be emotionally "short of breath." Not enough will happen in her lessons; the children will be full of expectations that remain unfulfilled; they will get restless and have a lot of questions that remain unanswered. In one of his last lectures to teachers, Rudolf Steiner called attention to the fact that sluggishness or apathy on the part of a teacher can lead to nervousness in the children later in life.[20]

We can try to understand this connection by imagining how restless and nervous we become if someone is telling us something boring in a monotonous voice, pausing between words to think of something else for a moment, and then droning on. We adults can push this aside inwardly so it doesn't affect us, but in the case of children, it can clearly lead to more serious consequences.

The great characteristics of the melancholic temperament, such as seriousness, clarity of thought and the ability to empathize, have a favorable effect on children; but when the melancholic becomes too focused on himself, too introverted and self-absorbed or prone to pessimism and pedantry, his preoccupation with himself can lead to an unhealthy egotism. If a parent or educator behaves like this, a cool mood will prevail that can grow into an atmosphere of icy reserve. Such people are easily irritated by children and are therefore constantly telling them what to do, criticizing them and demanding more; this cool emotional state will also take its toll. Emotional coldness will surround the child, and it is well known that its effects will be felt in the heart.

Continually demanding a pedantic and excessive attention to detail, which the child can never totally achieve, results in the child's feeling constantly restricted and unable to breathe freely. And this can lead to further dissatisfaction in our melancholic adult, which makes the atmosphere even more depressing for the child and can have an increasingly negative effect on her breathing. Rudolf Steiner commented that "through the teacher's letting his melancholic temperament loose," such experiences can lead to later irregularities in the child's breathing and circulation. This may sound extreme, but we can take it in as an interesting suggestion for observing on our own.

The optimism, liveliness and mobility of the sanguine educator will suit children very well as long as she does not give full vent to her temperament. If this does happen, we can imagine that she will mention things only briefly in class without going into enough detail; that she will deal only cursorily with the children's questions, answering them superficially and quickly moving on; that she will promise things for the next day but not keep her promises because she forgot, or never really meant, what she said; that she will not prepare her lessons sufficiently or follow them up adequately; that she is not truly interested in her pupils; and so on. Children want to learn; they want to be stimulated to ask questions, and they want answers they can ponder. They also want to learn about life's weightier issues, and how to become active citizens of the world. Instead of meeting this need, the overly sanguine teacher will tend to be too active, robbing the children of the opportunity to deal intensively with a topic themselves. This can have a harmful, paralyzing effect on the child.

If we can see things this way, we will comprehend the following statement by Rudolf Steiner: "Without self-education, the sanguine temperament of the teacher leads to a suppression of vitality, a suppression of the joy of life and of the forceful willpower that comes from an individual." In other words, the sanguine's excessive, volatile liveliness will not carry over to the children, but will cause the opposite tendency in them, potentially leading to a lack of vitality or initiative.

Ideas for Self-Education

It has become clear that any temperament that is not adequately controlled by the teacher or parent has effects on children that can even lead to illness. We must ask ourselves whether and how we can change anything about our main temperament. Rudolf Steiner spoke often about the necessity of self-education in educators: "We already sense that it cannot be that the educator simply says: temperament is congenital, and I cannot do anything to change it. First of all, that is not true, and secondly, if it were true, then the human race would have died out long ago as a result of incorrect education."[21]

First of all we need to discern which of the four temperaments— all of which are present in each of us—is the main one that we have trouble controlling. Then we need to consciously cultivate the temperament that stands in direct opposition. So if we are a choleric, we must try wherever possible to assume phlegmatic characteristics, seeking opportunities to remain calm and impassive. In addition, we may notice that a third temperament is only minimally developed in us, or not at all; we can focus our attention on it and try to strengthen it, gradually developing it in appropriate situations.

It is also well known that all artistic activities, whether playing music, painting, drawing, sculpting, etc., have a harmonizing effect on the temperaments. It was Rudolf Steiner's opinion that this kind of self-education and related ways of working on our temperaments should already be practiced during teacher training. How might such a process of self-education look?

The sanguine educator can start off by seriously attempting to complete all activities she begins, thus achieving greater perseverance. The phlegmatic can begin to develop interest in something that was previously completely insignificant for him. The melancholic will make inner progress when he not only feels empathy with others but begins to care for them in a practical way. The choleric should learn to control herself and plan on meeting, and dealing with, unexpected resistance.

These are all exercises we can rationally decide to undertake. But they will only slowly and minimally lead to noticeable results, because the qualities of the temperaments are based on very deep habits. If we practice regularly and persistently, we will notice results, but a completely different kind of self-education is still necessary to produce the kind of "wearing down" that leads to true control of our temperament.

An Exercise for the Sanguine

Rudolf Steiner also gave suggestions on this topic, which we can interpret as exercises.[22] If we observe that one of the temperaments is threatening to dominate us, it will not help to appeal to our conscience or reproach ourselves and regret that we are the way we are. We need to take action. If we notice that we have a lot of sanguine qualities, we need to "seek or create opportunities ourselves in which it is totally acceptable and even necessary to behave in a sanguine manner." So we should try to create situations in which brief interest is justified and called for. Whenever we are confronted with a wide range of rapidly changing sense impressions, we should experience only brief interest in them.

An example: Let's imagine that we are driving down a busy street in a big city. We receive a huge variety of impressions, so many that we can't be interested in all of them for more than a moment. This is a rich training ground for the sanguine.

What and how can she practice as she drives down the street? She looks here, she looks there, seeing lots of things that interest her and many that don't. This exercise now calls for her to consciously notice everything she sees over a period of a few minutes (one or two will suffice at first), and to quickly identify and record each sense impression: On the right there is a shoe store; next door a beauty salon; that woman is wearing a fashionable hat, the man next to her a sports coat; over there a car is going very fast, a Nissan; the policeman is watching it; that lamppost is not straight; a child is waiting on the curb; the traffic light is red; an old woman is crossing in front of me with a shopping bag, without a hat, in a light coat; somebody smells like perfume; over there is a porcelain shop – in the store window I see coffee pots, cups and saucers, plates, etc. One impression after the other, which she observes and names with no inner connection. The faster she can do this, the more effective the exercise. She should look at and name more than sixty things per minute.

This is an excellent exercise for a sanguine person. It is strenuous, so she will do it only for a short time in city traffic. But it is also sufficient. She should plan on doing it for a few minutes daily for a long time, one to three months, then take a break and start again later, preferably over the course of years, and not just in city traffic! She will experience countless opportunities to practice this. She could also closely observe her surroundings for a few minutes while hiking in the woods, registering all the sense impressions and paying special attention to everything that she finds barely interesting. In addition to sights, she should notice what she smells, hears, feels. Rudolf Steiner said that if she only "works at it long enough," she will experience "that this temperament develops the force to change itself."

This detailed example reveals the basic concept of self-education: We treat like with like, but we ourselves are the ones who must create the appropriate occasions. No one is forcing us to do so—we do it out of our own free will. We will notice successes if we do this exercise repeatedly and manage to be consciously and willfully sanguine. The same holds true for the other exercises described below. One day we may notice that we are exercising our temperament *voluntarily*. When this happens, our will has united with our temperament; in the long run, our temperament will now be more receptive to our will when it threatens to do its own thing.

An Exercise for the Phlegmatic

If we have phlegmatic tendencies and only a few interests, it will be good for us "to occupy ourselves as much as possible with quite uninteresting things, to surround ourselves with many sources of ennui, so that we are thoroughly bored." We should seek out occupations deserving of apathy, in which we can let ourselves feel totally apathetic. With this temperament, too, we are working with what is there, not what is missing. Let's illustrate this with an example of a pastime that will let us experience how dismally boring it would be, even for a phlegmatic, to have to do it again and again.

Let us imagine a jigsaw puzzle with two thousand pieces which, when finished, will depict a monotonous landscape with a lot of blue sky (about half of it). After the phlegmatic has put together the first half, a thousand blue pieces are still lying on the table, and they all look alike! Finding the right pieces takes forever and is boring, but so is the finished product! The phlegmatic will take a long time to finish this project. And in case he has not yet bored himself silly, he will need to take it apart again later and start over from scratch—and then repeat this again and again.

This exercise is especially effective for a phlegmatic when he himself has to think up the activity that will bore him, and do it precisely for that purpose. It is crucial that he take hold of his temperament with his own willpower; in time, he will get used to doing so. Then he will also become able to pull himself together and tackle his excessive apathy in particular life situations. That is the significant fruit of this boring exercise.

Before we take a look at the suggestions for self-education for the two remaining temperaments, we should call to mind an important and interesting aspect in the comparison of the melancholic and the choleric: The melancholic is a good thinker who doesn't have an easy time making the transition to practical work, while the choleric acts spontaneously without having thought things through sufficiently beforehand.

An Exercise for the Melancholic

If we have a strong melancholic tendency, we will observe that we like to think carefully about everything, including things that we intend to put into action. Because of all the brooding, we may have trouble taking the action. As previously mentioned, Hippocrates discovered that in such cases the secretion of bile darkened to a black color (*melan chole* = black bile). (Interestingly, this happens in the same organ that makes cholerics especially active!) The main thing is for us to be able to take action, so that "what one possesses of pain and the capacity for suffering is diverted to outer objects" and we don't sink into self-pity. We should "create legitimate outer obstacles" for ourselves and use our abilities to overcome them. In other words: We should look for suffering in the world around us, and become active there.

Here is an example: Let us imagine that our melancholic is standing at a window—behind a curtain, of course, so no one can see him—and looking down at the street. He observes a woman returning from shopping, loaded down with all sorts of bags. He feels sorry for her, knowing that she lives way up on the third or fourth floor. She will have to walk up all those stairs, carrying all that weight! He can't understand why nobody offers to help carry her bags; he is very disappointed by this. "She has grown children who could even do her shopping for her! What's going to happen when she gets even older and can hardly walk? I wonder if I'll be in the same situation someday, when I'm her age?" Our melancholic is painfully affected.

This monologue reveals noble sympathy and depth of feeling, as well as criticism of others who aren't helping the old woman. The last sentence reveals that in his case, self-pity also enters into it. How might his painful feelings be channeled outward in a case like this? The melancholic could avoid all thoughts about himself and completely immerse himself in sympathy for the poor woman, which could give rise to the thought: "I would like to help her!" In this way he could bring himself to do something concrete, to act! He will make great strides when, instead of considering what *others* should be doing in a case like this, he asks himself what he could do for this person. He *himself* could decide to help by carrying her bags, or even by going shopping for her and lightening her load in other ways! That would distract him from himself, allowing him to overcome a lot of his surplus temperament.

Any such form of service to his fellow man will be of great significance for him and his inner well-being, but he must pursue it out of his own free will. There are also many professions in which his valuable qualities are particularly desirable.

An Exercise for the Choleric

If we notice strong choleric traits in ourselves, such as having a short fuse, reacting violently or just being irritable, there are two things we should pay particular attention to.

First, before beginning a task, we should realize clearly that unexpected things may happen, and that they might get us upset. In contrast to our melancholic colleagues, we like to act immediately and think about it afterward, so it would be good if before beginning a task, we could plan to immediately interrupt what we're doing and suddenly decide to do something else instead. It should be something quite simple: We should seek out "insignificant things that offer no resistance."

As long as we are still completely calm and in the planning phase, this suggestion might seem quite doable. But if we are already angry, we must somehow try—and this is the second suggestion—to release our bottled-up, surplus energies in a place where we will cause no damage. We have to "try to find as many things as possible that require little force to be overcome" and "to bring this force to expression in the strongest way upon insignificant events and facts."

Some cholerics hang a punching bag in their basement or workroom, and when they sense they are about to get angry and feel their muscles tensing up, they go there to release extra energy by forcefully punching the bag. Afterward they feel completely relieved, as well as glad that they caused no damage in the family and insulted nobody. This example shows us that it is important to be active with our limbs to release tension or cramping.

A further example from everyday life: A mother is growing increasingly frustrated because her children are making a lot of noise. If she is almost at the point of exploding, she could go into the next room and punch an upholstered chair or pound a mattress. She will quickly notice how relieved she feels afterward. In this way the fiery forces of the choleric are allowed free rein in a very direct way, so she is spared from destroying an object or even beating up on other people, as some tend to do when they have lost control of themselves.

In general, a choleric approaches a task quickly and tackles it energetically, but doesn't think far enough ahead and can thus run into obstacles, which frustrate her mightily. She may get furious and even throw a tantrum. A choleric who is this easily excited needs to plan in advance what she will do if things don't go the way she assumes they will.

Then, if difficulties do arise and thing aren't working out, she should stop and do what she had planned beforehand: tackle something insignificant that offers no resistance. It's a good idea to hold off on the task for a while, sit down and do something simple such as reading the paper for a few minutes, going outside and counting to ten, or going down into the basement to look for another tool. This will give her the space and time she needs to think through the process again and decide on the logical next step.

The choleric must learn to think about things in advance and admit that she might make mistakes. Of course, that is precisely what she has trouble doing, though she doesn't want to admit it!

Thus, by venting her choleric qualities on resistances that are real but easy to overcome, she will hopefully be able to admit to the absurdity of her temperamental outburst and stop for a moment. With time, her thinking will win over her temperament, and at some point she will even be able to control her most serious outbursts. We have paid special attention to the choleric since there is no other temperament that can destroy a social relationship as quickly.

We have seen that each of us has the possibility for self-education with respect to our dominant temperament, if only we wish to exercise it. By consciously allowing our mind access to our temperament, we also ultimately enable it to prevail. We are actually doing this for our fellow human beings, especially for the children, who would otherwise suffer from the effects of our uncontrolled temperaments.

In one of the lectures by Rudolf Steiner that we have cited frequently, we find a few sentences with which we can now close our chapter on self-education: "It is good if a temperament is developed in the right way during childhood, but often the adult himself has to take his education and development in hand later in life. Indeed, as long as the temperaments are held in normal bounds, they represent what makes life beautiful, varied, and great. How dull would life be if all people were alike with regard to temperament!"

12. Concluding Thoughts

My purpose in writing this book was to help readers experience
and understand the temperaments and learn to deal with them
practically in everyday life, but above all to learn to *love them all*.
Taken together they constitute a whole, an entity, that exists in
every human being. We have traveled down a long path together;
first we vividly pictured the differences between temperaments,
and then we worked out the basic underlying ideas in order to
find approaches for dealing practically with children in school and
at home, as well as with ourselves.

During my seminars or after my lectures, the question has often been asked why there are four and not five or more temperaments. I hope the material in these chapters has explained this sufficiently, and that readers can now answer this for themselves. Nevertheless, I would like to address it further: One could speak of a fifth temperament and put it in the middle of the cross on the diagram. This would be the "ability to transform oneself," which we can only acquire through practice, by learning to slip into the four different temperaments time and again! When we have developed this into a deeply seated habit, we could perhaps compare the ability to transform ourselves to a temperament.

There is hardly any other profession that lends itself better to doing this than that of the educator! Teachers are confronted with new riddles and mysteries in every child, and in order to solve these they must be constant learners. This is precisely what children are seeking—not people who feel they are close to perfection, but people who learn anew from every opportunity and want to develop themselves further through self-education. In this context, we as educators should be especially grateful to those children who do not give us an easy time but present us with challenging tasks that contribute to our inner growth.

We can compare everything that has been described here to an orchestra playing a symphony with four movements, directed by a conductor. If we look at the various instruments and the four parts of the music, we can draw connections with the temperaments. When we hear the individual movements, one is always noticeably slower (phlegmatic) and one definitely faster (sanguine). We will not categorize the other two movements because the composers surely did not consider this aspect when composing. We can now observe a good conductor who no longer needs to look at the score because she has internalized the harmonies of all the instruments, and already knows which instrumental group she will signal to come in next, or to play more loudly or softly. Everything depends on her and her abilities.

If our life resembles the playing of a symphony, could we not compare ourselves to an orchestra conductor who emphasizes the temperament best suited for different situations and lets it "play"? In our lives, opportunities arise constantly that call for the friendliness and inner flexibility of the sanguine temperament, while others can be handled only by the earnestness and clear thinking of the melancholic. When determination and willpower are called for, the "conductor" within us will turn to the choleric temperament, knowing that in other situations only the tranquility and faithful staying power of the phlegmatic can lead to success. Through this metaphor we can again clearly recognize how important it is to harmonize the four temperaments within ourselves. If we haven't yet succeeded in doing this, we could say: The individual instruments in the orchestra are not yet tuned correctly to each other so that, for example, the trumpets are drowning out everybody else, or the violins are playing much too quietly.

Since we imagined at the beginning of our observations how different children greet their class teacher in the morning, it seems fitting here at the end to attempt a fourfold farewell to our readers.

The melancholic puts himself in the readers' shoes and asks himself serious questions: Did I expect too much of them? Was everything understandable? Did I disappoint them? What should I do if they expected something completely different? Farewell.

The choleric is a person of action, not words, and is done quickly: That's it! Thanks for reading! Be sure to practice!

The phlegmatic looks forward to some peace and quiet. Good – now he has said enough – it was a lot of work – but now he'll get a break and will be able to recover ... He can get comfortable at home, put his feet up, and read the whole thing over again.

The sanguine is always thinking of new things and doesn't know when to stop saying goodbye: Oh, how great, the book is already done. Yes, I really enjoyed writing it all down for you. I didn't even know beforehand that I could write so much. I kept on getting all these new ideas. But now I do have to close. It would make me really happy if you laughed a lot while reading this. I love to laugh, too. Laughing is good for your health, they say. How great that you're done reading now, because you'll have time for your kids again. They'll be happy about that. Say hi to them from me – and to your better half, too. Goodbye, and thanks a lot for sticking it out!

Endnotes

1   Peter Lipps, *Temperamente und Pädagogik. Eine Darstellung für den Unterricht an der Waldorfschule*, Stuttgart, 1998.

2   Especially impressive: Peter Lipps, loc.cit. (Note 1), pp. 20, 30, 45, 53.

3   Rudolf Steiner, *Discussions with Teachers*, GA 295, Dornach, 1984, First Seminar Discussion of August 21, 1919.

4   Rudolf Steiner, *The Four Temperaments*, translated by Frances Dawson from the German original, *The Mystery of the Human Temperaments*, text compiled by C. Englert-Faye in wording from several lectures, Basel 1967.

5   Op. cit., Steiner, Seminar discussion. (Note 3).

6   Ibid. (Note 4), p. 31ff. The following quotes also come from these lectures.

7   Ibid., p. 39ff.

8   Op. cit., Steiner, Seminar discussion. (Note 3).

9   Rudolf Steiner, *The Kingdom of Childhood*, GA 311, Dornach, 1989, Lecture of August 15, 1924, p. 70.

10 Op. cit., Steiner, Second Seminar discussion. (Note 3).

11 Edmund Hillary, *High Adventure: The True Story of the First Ascent of Everest*, Oxford University Press, 2003.

12 Judy and Tashi Tenzing, *Tenzing Norgay and the Sherpas of Everest*, Camden, ME, 2001.

13 Op. cit., Lipps. (Note 1), p. 240ff.

14 See Rudolf Steiner, *Practical Course for Teachers*, GA 294, Dornach, 1990, Lecture of August 28, 1919; also the bibliographic references in Helmut Eller, *Der Klassenlehrer an der Waldorfschule [The Class Teacher at the Waldorf School]*, Stuttgart, 2007.

15 See Manfred von Mackensen, "Fire Variations," in *Fire – Lime – Metals*, Kassel, 1995.

16 See Erika Dühnfort, *Der Sprachbau als Kunstwerk. Grammatik im Rahmen der Waldorfpädagogik*, Stuttgart, 1997, p. 269ff.

17 Udo von Renzenbrink, *Ernährung unserer Kinder. Gesundes Wachstum, Konzentration, soziales Verhalten, Willensbildung*, Stuttgart, 2004, p. 129ff.

18 Ibid.

19 Gerda Scheer-Krüger, *Das offenbare Geheimnis der Temperamente. Studien zu einem vertieften Verständnis der Temperamentskunde Rudolf Steiners*, Dornach 1996, Ch. 2.

20 Rudolf Steiner, *The Essentials of Education*, GA 308, Dornach, 1986, Lecture of April 8, 1924.

21 Op. cit., Steiner, *The Four Temperaments*. (Note 4).

22 Ibid.

Made in the USA
Lexington, KY
13 September 2018